TRUE LOVE
KNOWS NO BOUNDARIES

Copyright © 2015 by Dennis Corrigan

Cover design by Joe Scorsone

ISBN13: 978-1-936936-08-3
Library of Congress Control Number: 2015937175

Published by Avventura Press
Eynon, PA 18403

Printed in the USA
First printing May 2015

TRUE LOVE
KNOWS NO BOUNDARIES

DRAWINGS BY DENNIS CORRIGAN

Avventura Press

from the artist...

Most of these drawings were created during the summer and fall of 2014, with me curled into a couch corner in a semi-fetal position, armed with mechanical pencils, kneaded erasers, and a few tech pens. I was kind of burnt out on art in general, but had to keep making at least something. The results were a return to a kind of minimalist line drawing style, with an emphasis on humor, composition, and lunacy.

Most of the drawings first evolved on blank paper as random lines and scribbles that would gradually suggest forms, characters and compositions. The titles were developed as the work progressed, or after it was finished, or not at all, as some seemed to be title-resistant.

Technically speaking, the making of this work is very dry and often boring, and tense. Once all the line work in pencil is completed, it is followed by a very controlled inking and strengthening of these lines. This involves the wearing of two pairs of reading glasses and remaining as still and steady as possible for a couple of hours at a time.

Once this stage is completed, it is time to design and apply ink to the areas to be stippled. This provides a kind of graphic anchor and contrast to the simpler line work. And then the drawing is finished.

It's strange, but I think most artists go through a process of being both excited and afraid when starting a new work, and then totally doubting it in the middle stage, and not sure about its merits when the work is completed. Me too. But I'm happy to say that when viewing the drawings contained in this collection, far removed from the time of their creation, that I really like them. And I hope that they will provide a small mother lode of laughter for a wide range of viewers.

DENNIS CORRIGAN

"TROUBLE IN THE VESTIBULE"

"FRIENDLY NEIGHBOR, JUST PASSING BY"

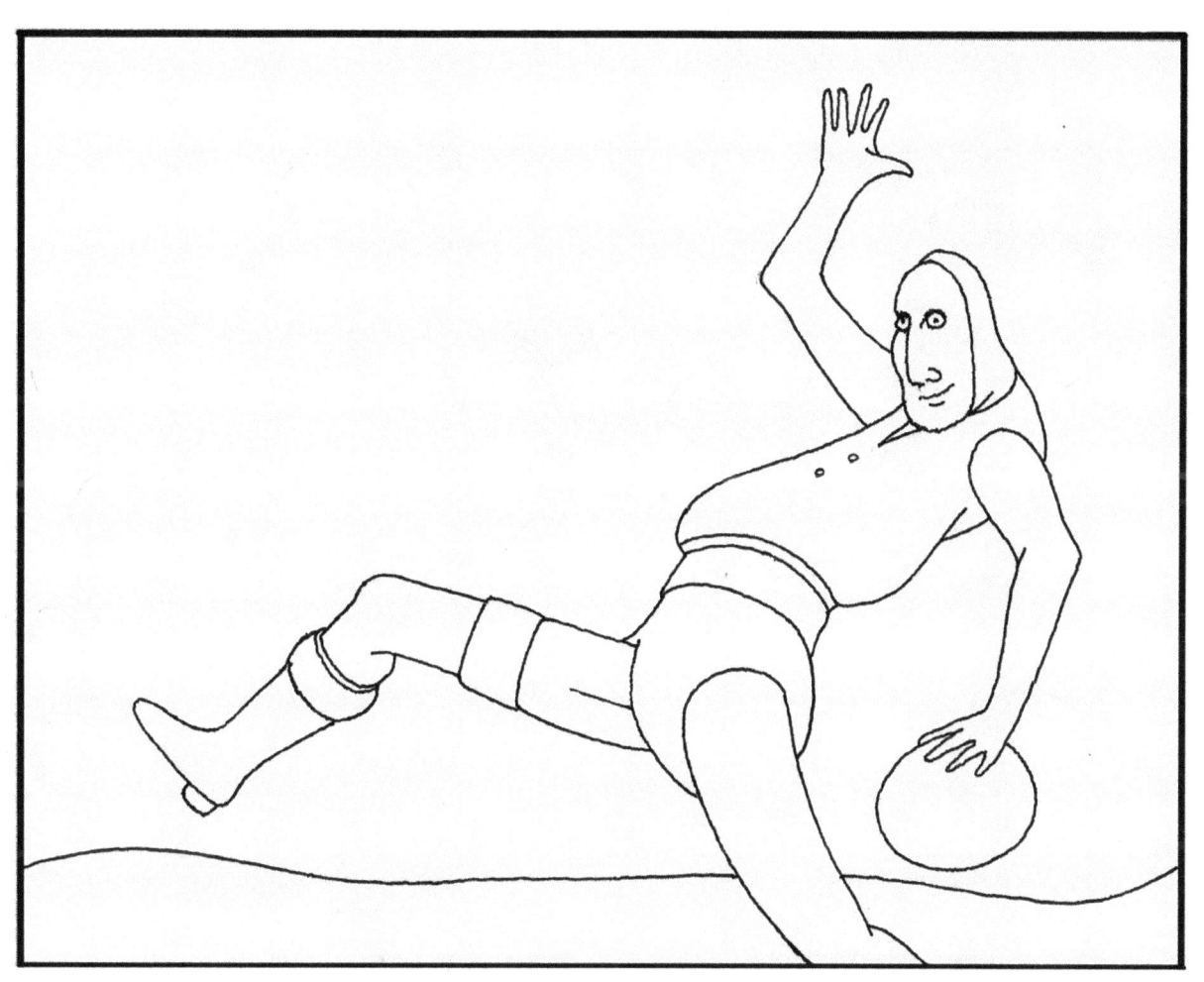

"CLUMSY WOMAN WITH ROVING EYE, BOWLING IN THE DESERT"

"WINGED JACKASS TORMENTING A SIMPLE POLYP"

"MAN FORCING A MUTANT TO SNIFF HIS SHOE"

"LEVITATING AN ANTIPASTO"

"TAIL END OF THE MEAT AND MEAT BYPRODUCTS PARADE"

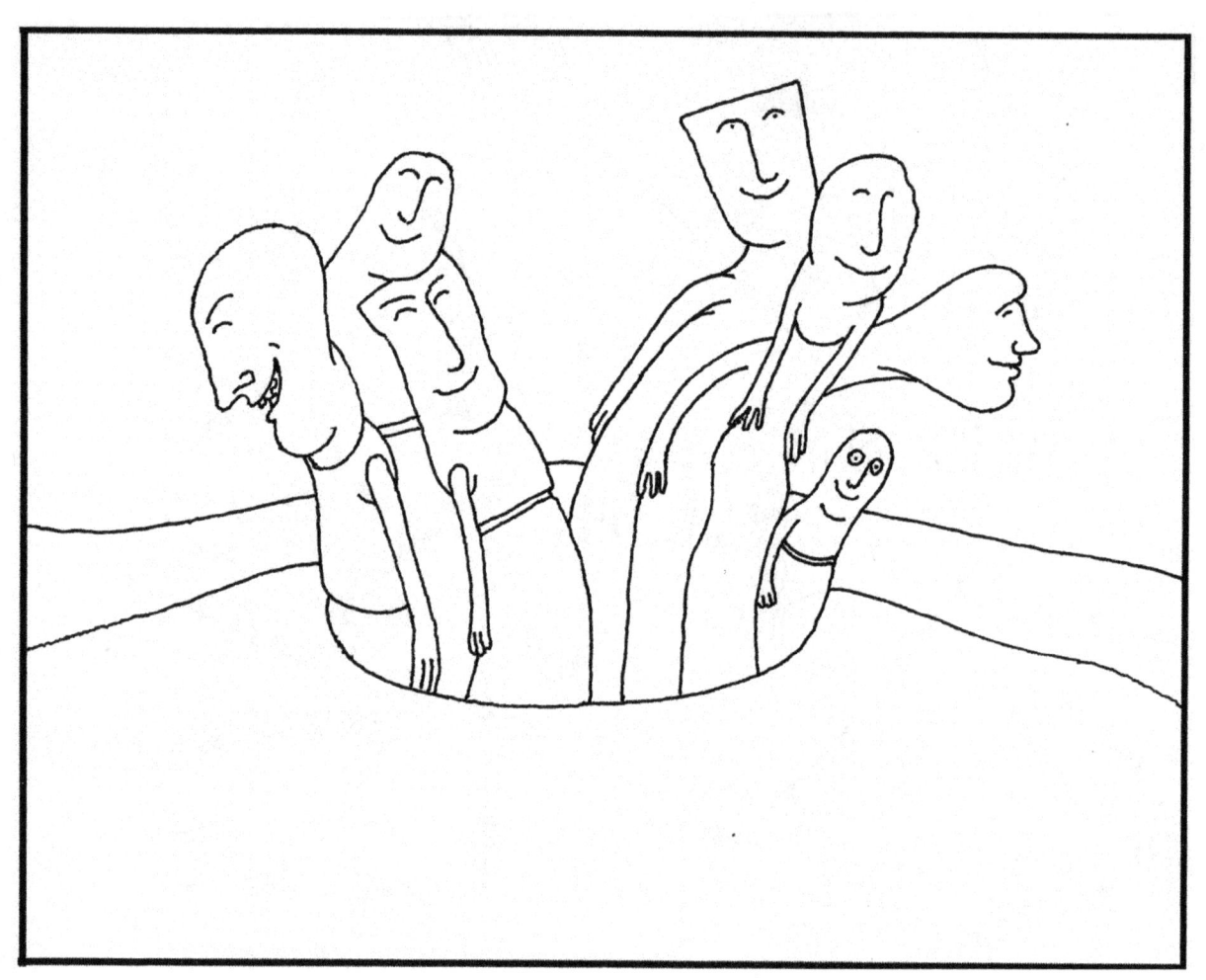

"A HOLE FULL OF HAPPINESS"

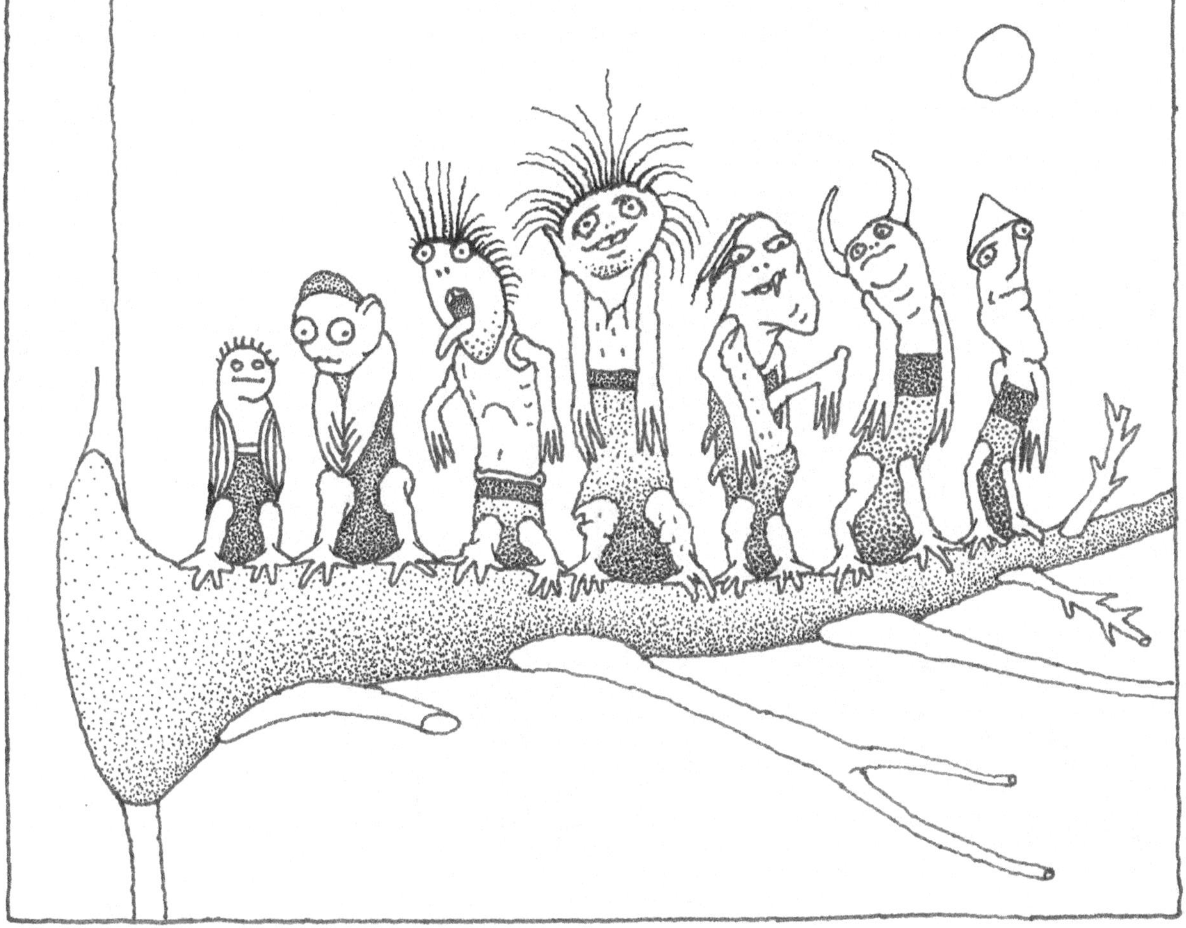

"BRANCH MANAGERS"

"DAD TAUGHT HIMSELF TO STEER THE FAMILY SEDAN WITH HIS ENORMOUS, STICKY TONGUE"

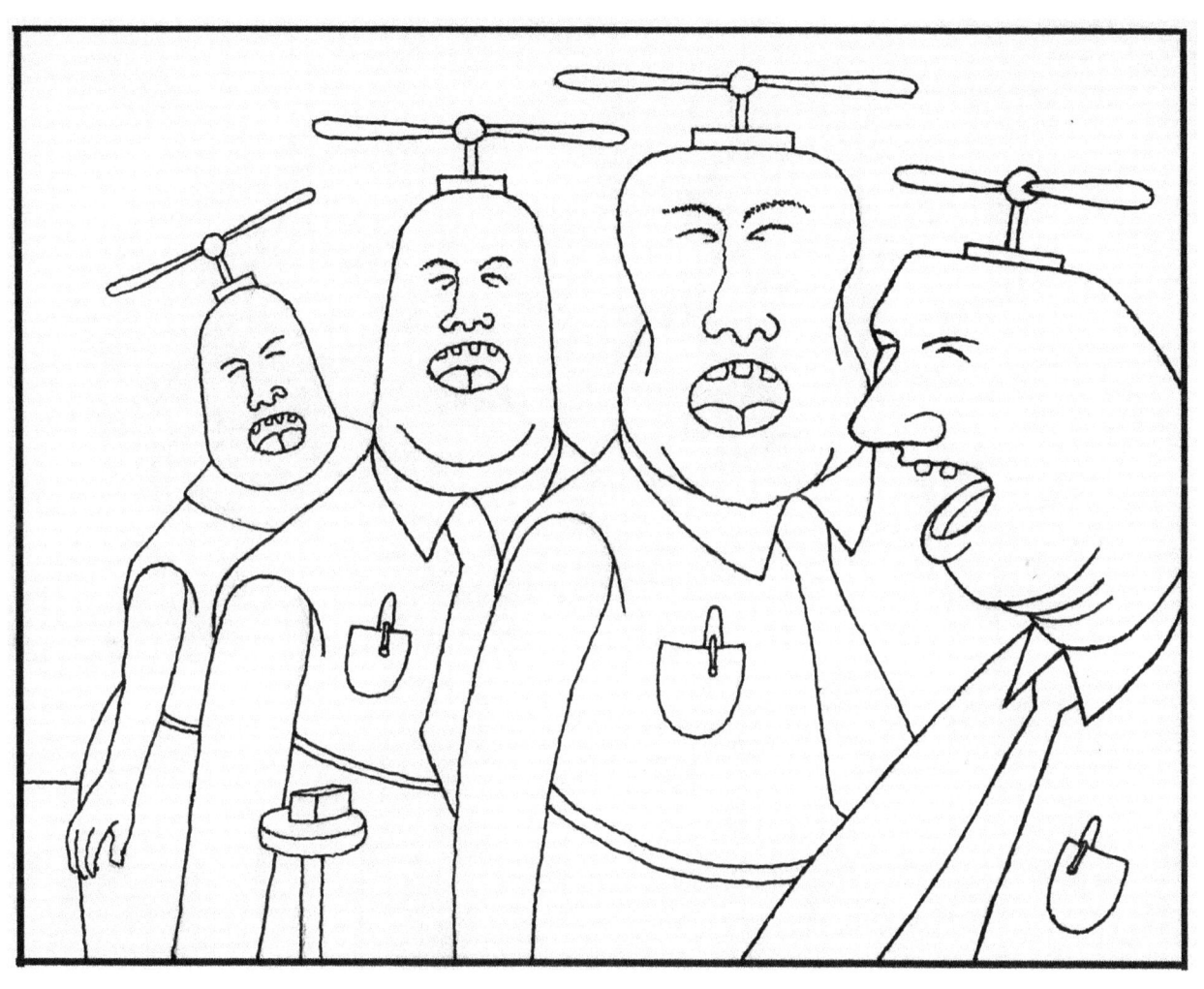

"FAT GUYS, WITH PROPELLORS, LAUGHING AT A STICK OF BUTTER"

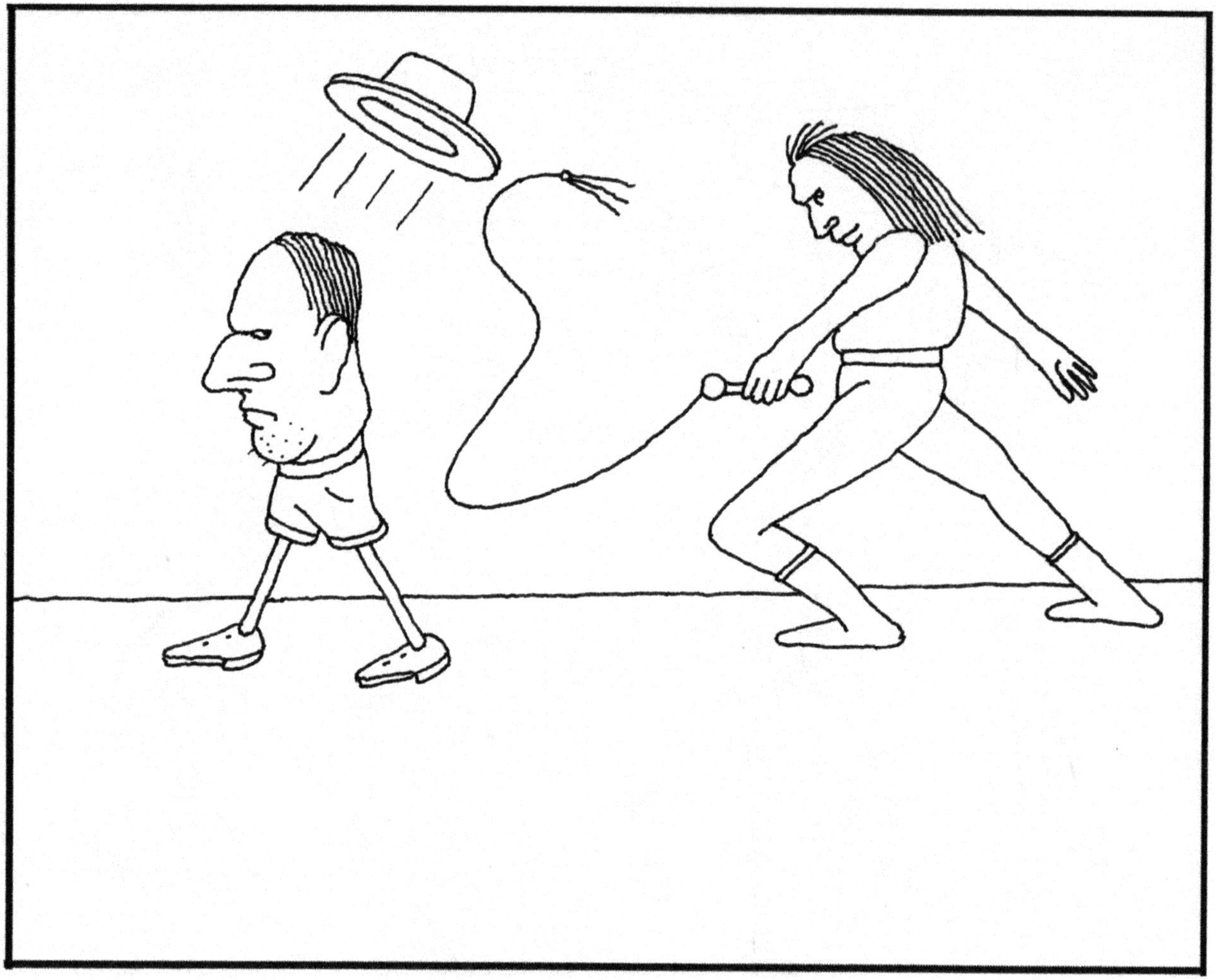

"BULLWHIP SURPRISE"

"STRANGE LITTLE MEN FROM PLUTO FORCED MICHAEL TO DO UNSPEAKABLE THINGS"

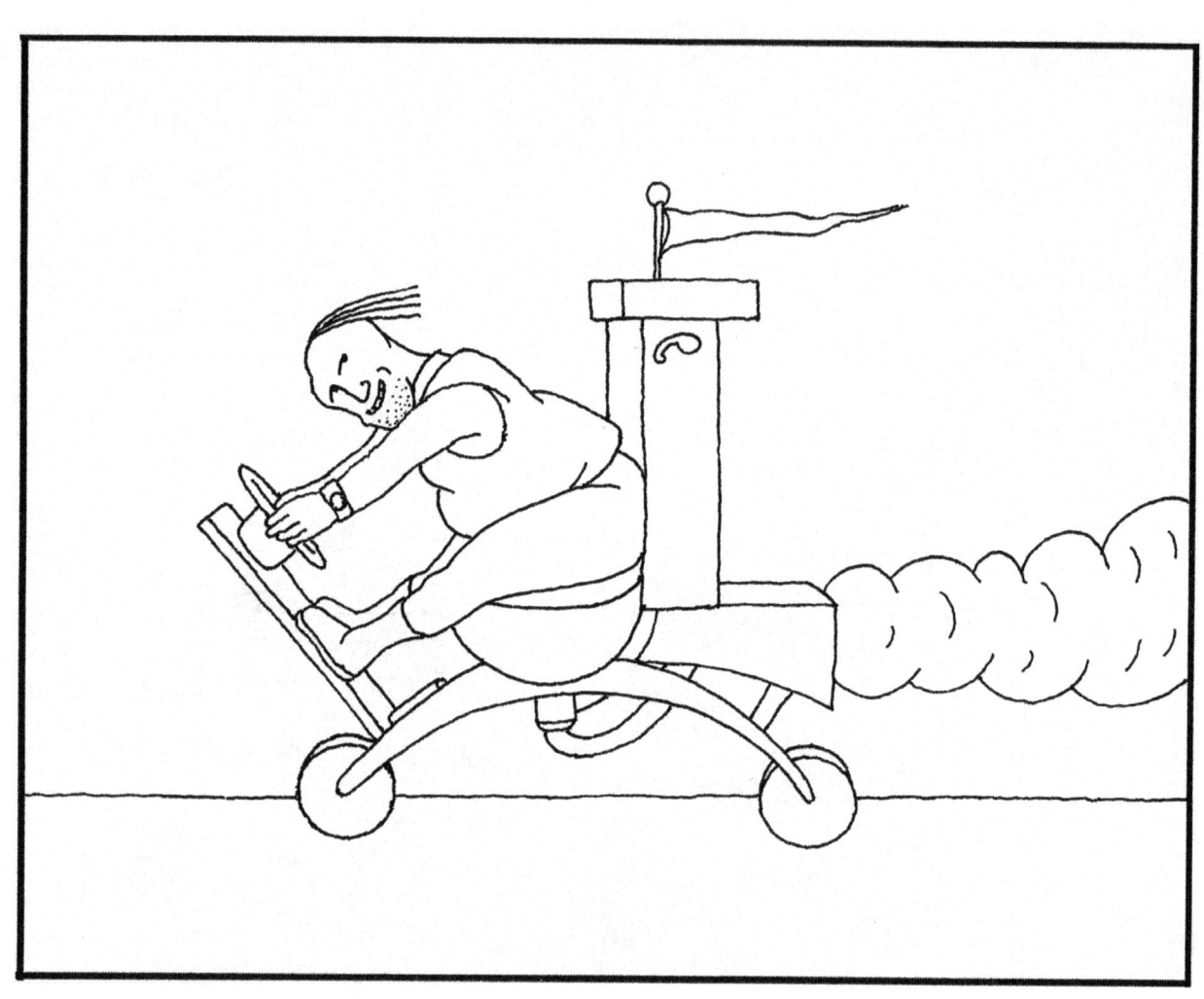

"GOD BLESS TOILET POWER"

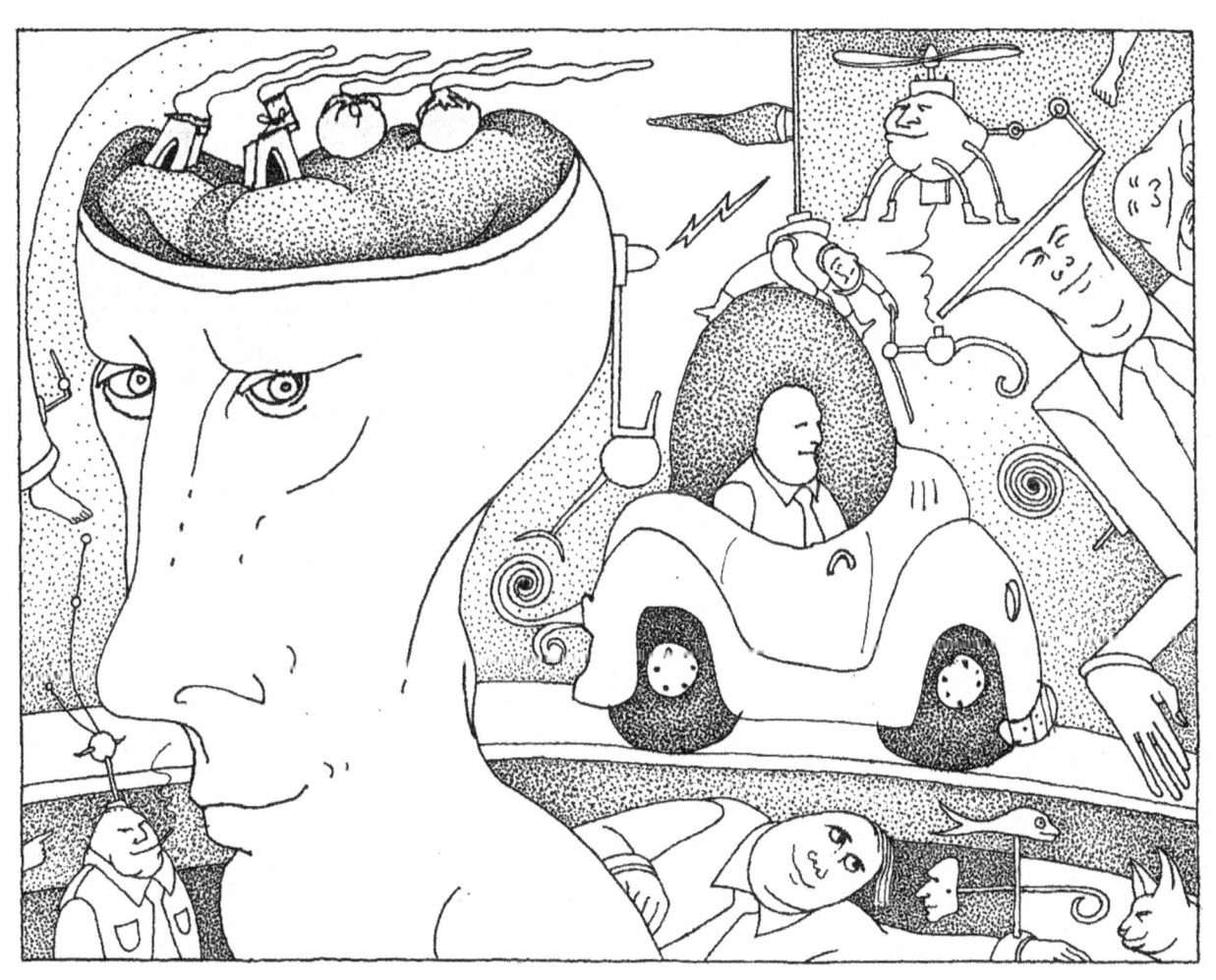

"YOUR GUESS IS AS GOOD AS MINE"

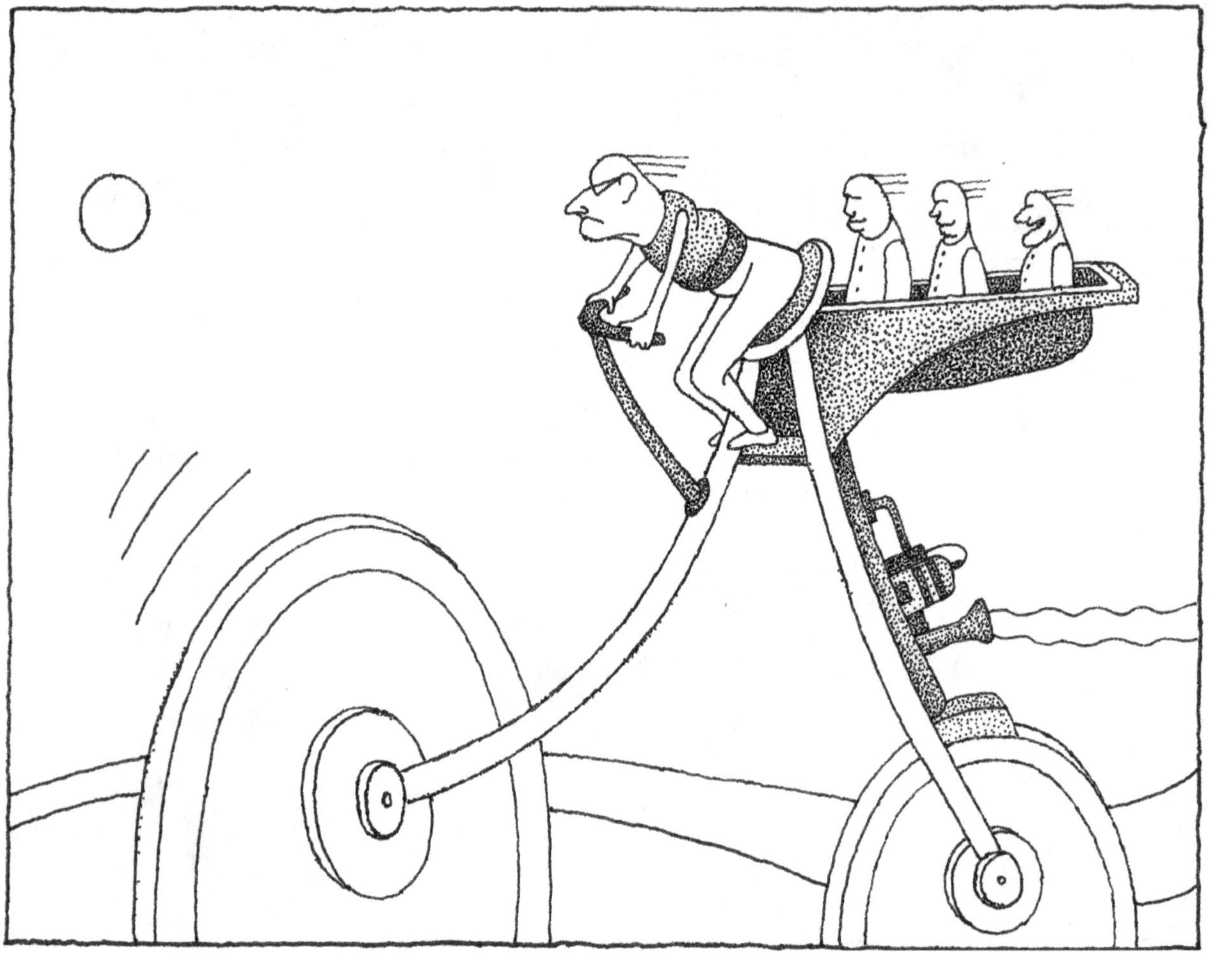

"LATE FOR MASS"

"IT WAS REALLY HARD TO HAVE FUN WHEN THE KRETCHMYER BROTHERS CAME TO TOWN"

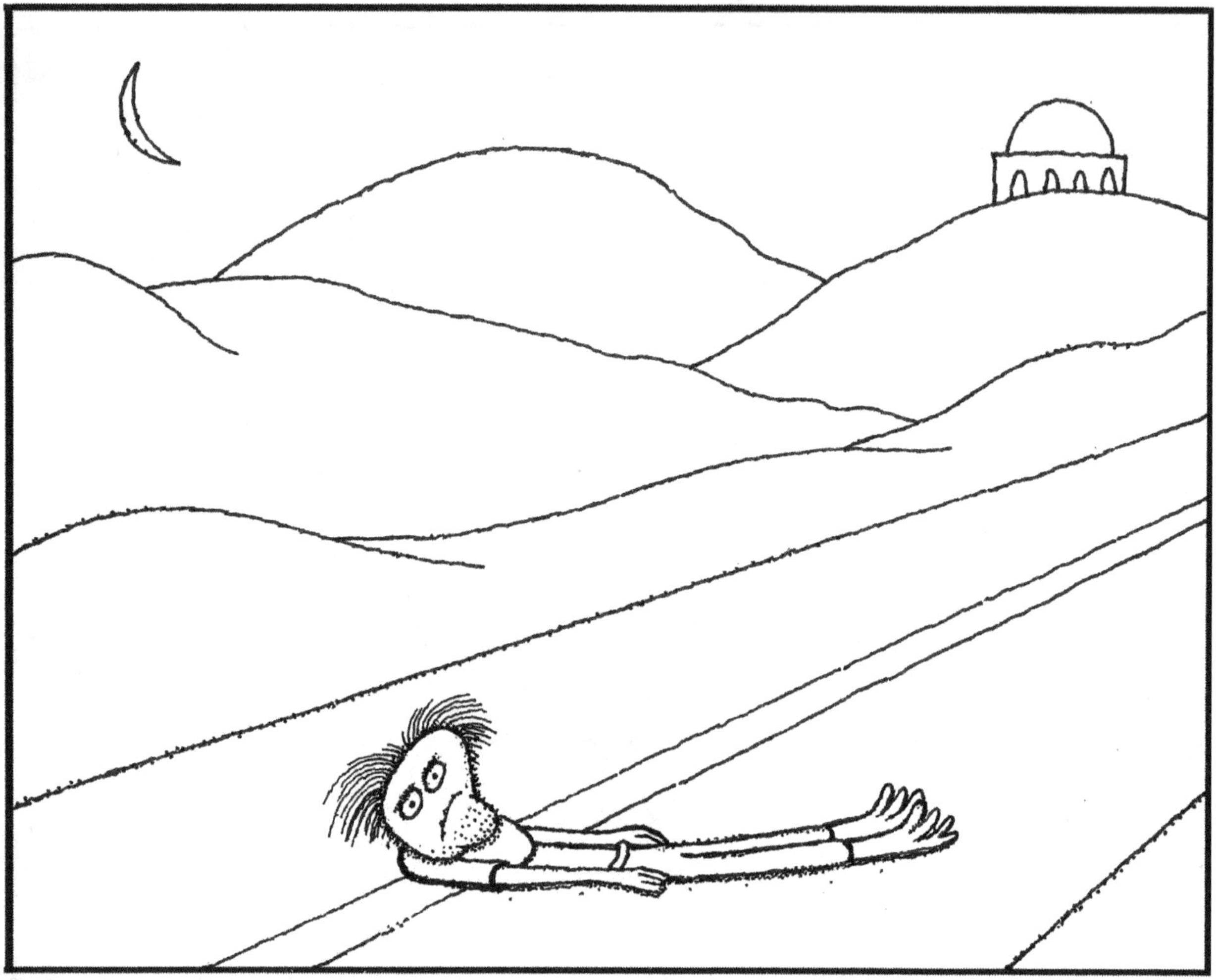

"WAITING FOR TRAFFIC"

"THE FEEDING OF DR. ABERNATHY"

"A HUGE AND HIDEOUS FLOATING BUTT BEDEVILS YOUNG SAINT NICK"

"PEOPLE RARELY PAID ATTENTION WHEN POINTING GEORGE DID HIS POINTING"

"NUDE MAN WITH MYSTERIOUS OBJECT"

"PROFESSOR HUGERNOT EXPLAINS HIS PREDICAMENT BEFORE THE GRIEVANCE COMMITTEE"

"NO PIZZA LIKE A SANCTIFIED PIZZA"

"AFTER MOM BECAME DAD, WE LIVED ON NOTHING BUT MARSHMALLOWS AND CROUTONS"

"PENNSYLVANIA DOUCHE SPOKEN HERE"

"TEACHING WILLIE TO DRIVE"

"CUBE-HEADED LUNATIC HOLDING UP A LEMONADE STAND"

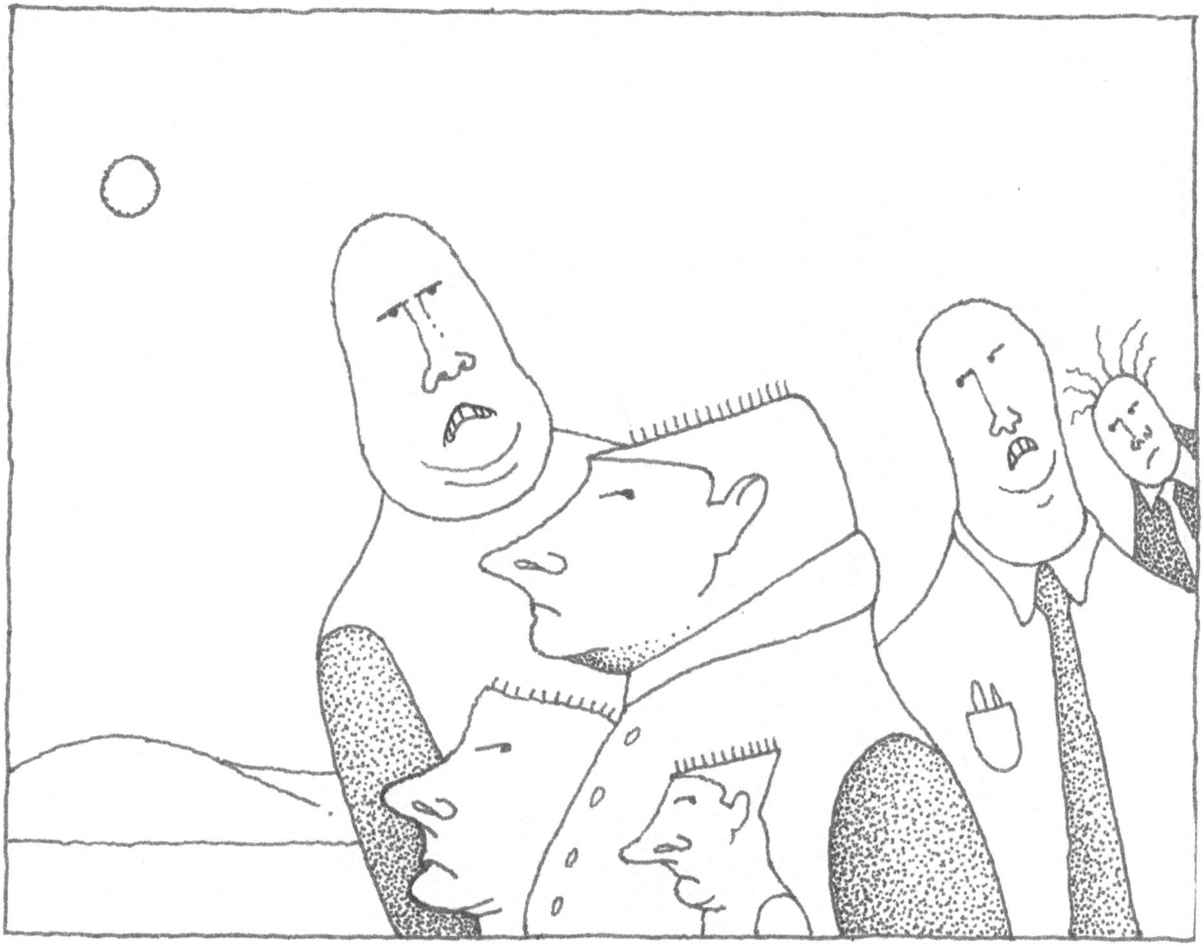

"MEN DETECTING A STENCH"

"THE BATTLE BETWEEN GOOD AND NOT SO GOOD"

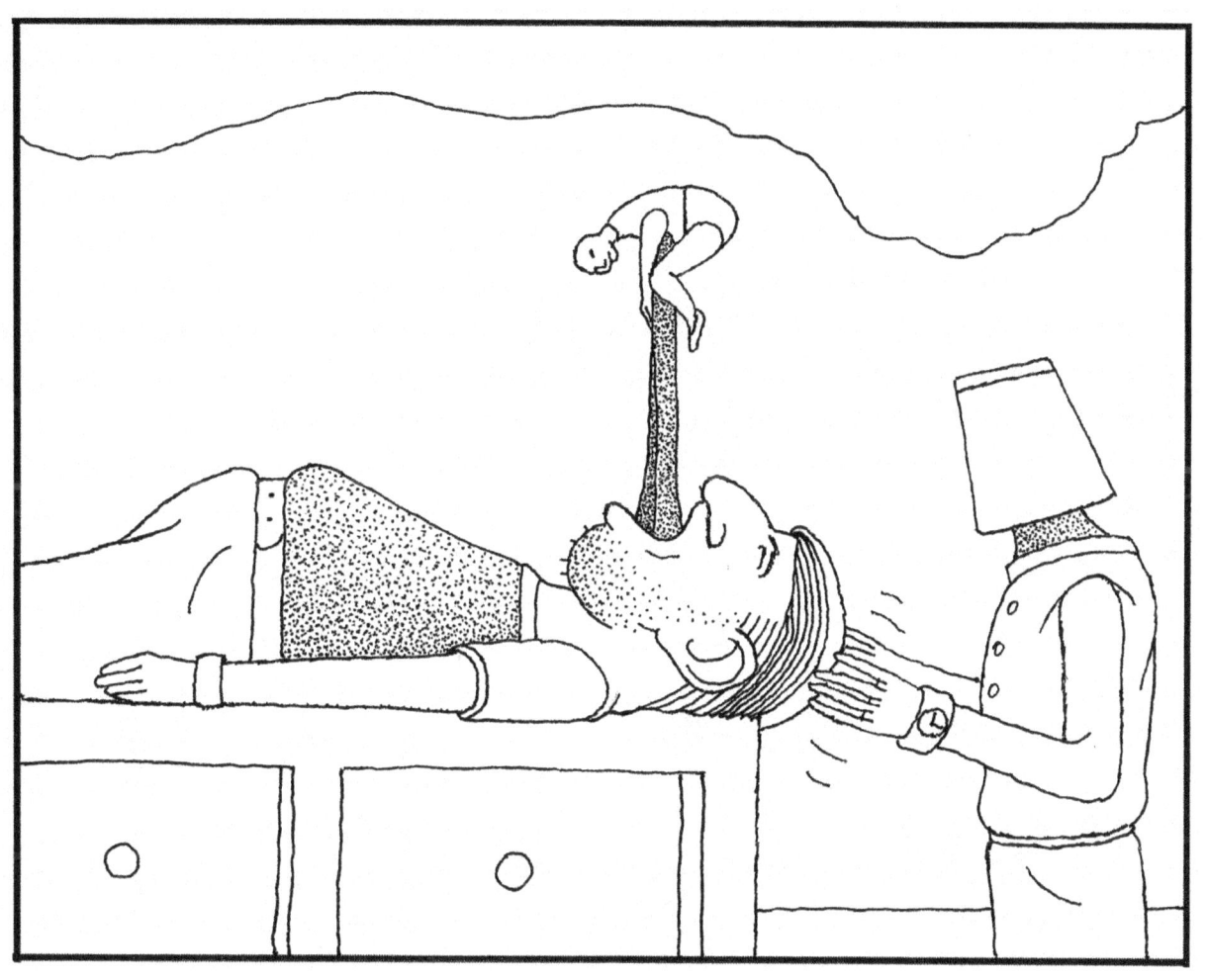

"PROFESSOR ARNSWORTH SUPPORTS A TINY COLLEAGUE ON HIS ATROCIOUS TONGUE WHILE A MYSTERIOUS PERSON SEARCHES FOR LICE"

"AN ABNORMAL PRIMATE TRIES TO PURCHASE SHY BENJAMIN'S SPECIAL HAT"

"DIRTY ALBERT LICKS THE BACK OF FRANK'S HEAD DESPITE MR. FONG'S DISAPPROVAL"

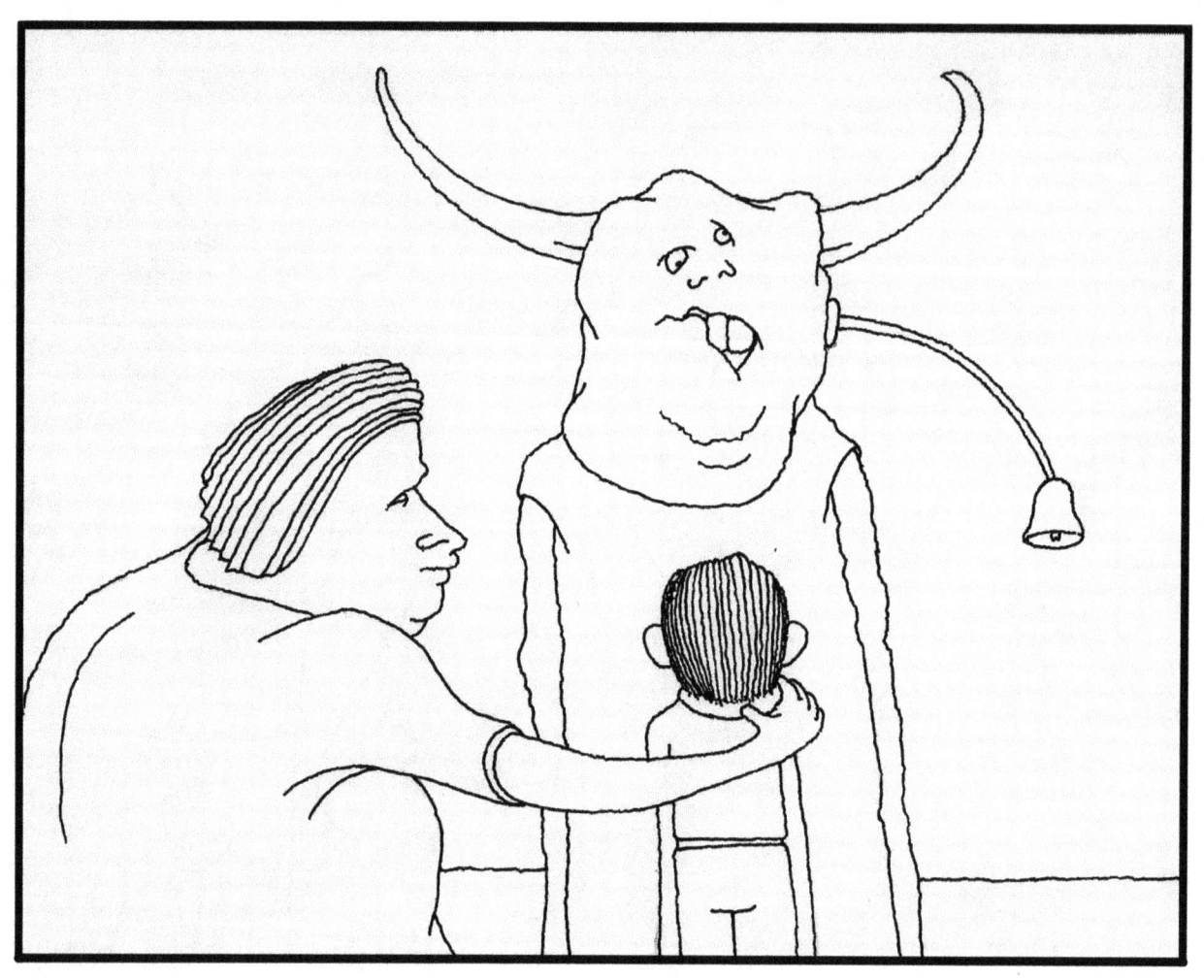

"BILLIE GETS TO MEET HIS REAL FATHER FOR THE FIRST TIME"

"THE STRANGER ON MY TOILET"

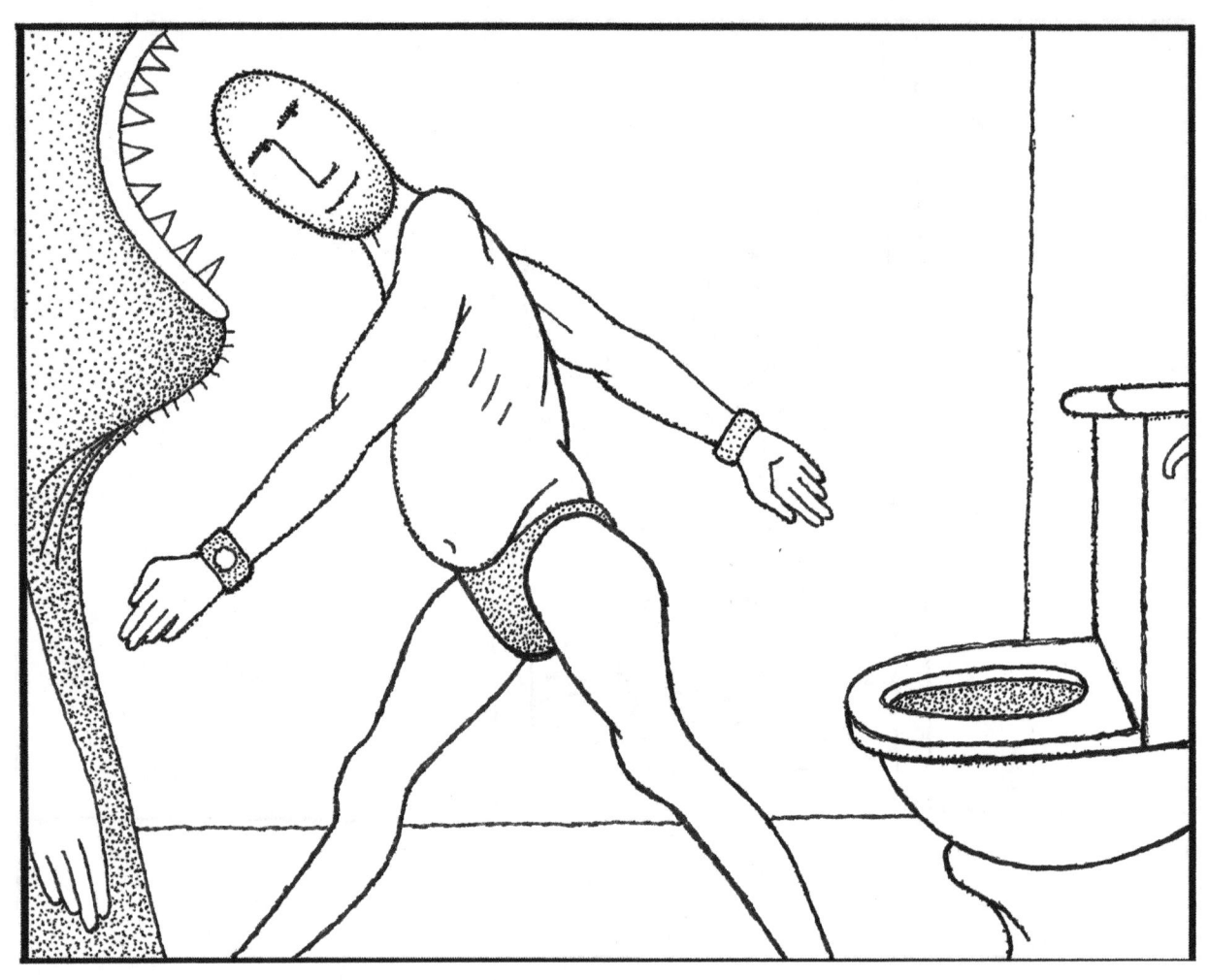

"FRESH FROM THE WARM EMBRACE OF AN ANTIQUE TOILET, SENATOR BLANCHARD STRIDES DIRECTLY INTO THE JAWS OF A DILEMMA"

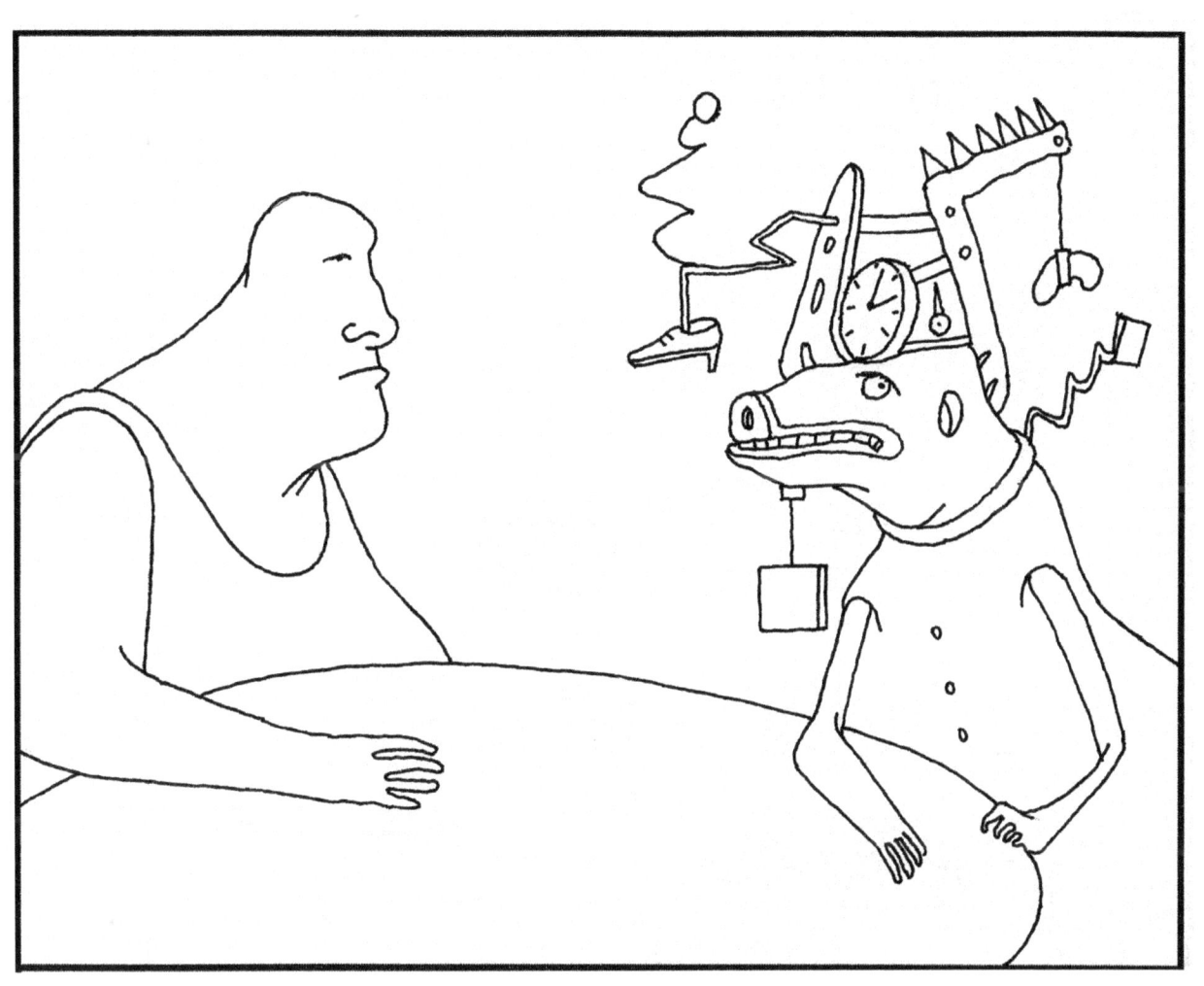

"SIMPLE IGNORANCE STARES DOWN A COMPLEX ENIGMA"

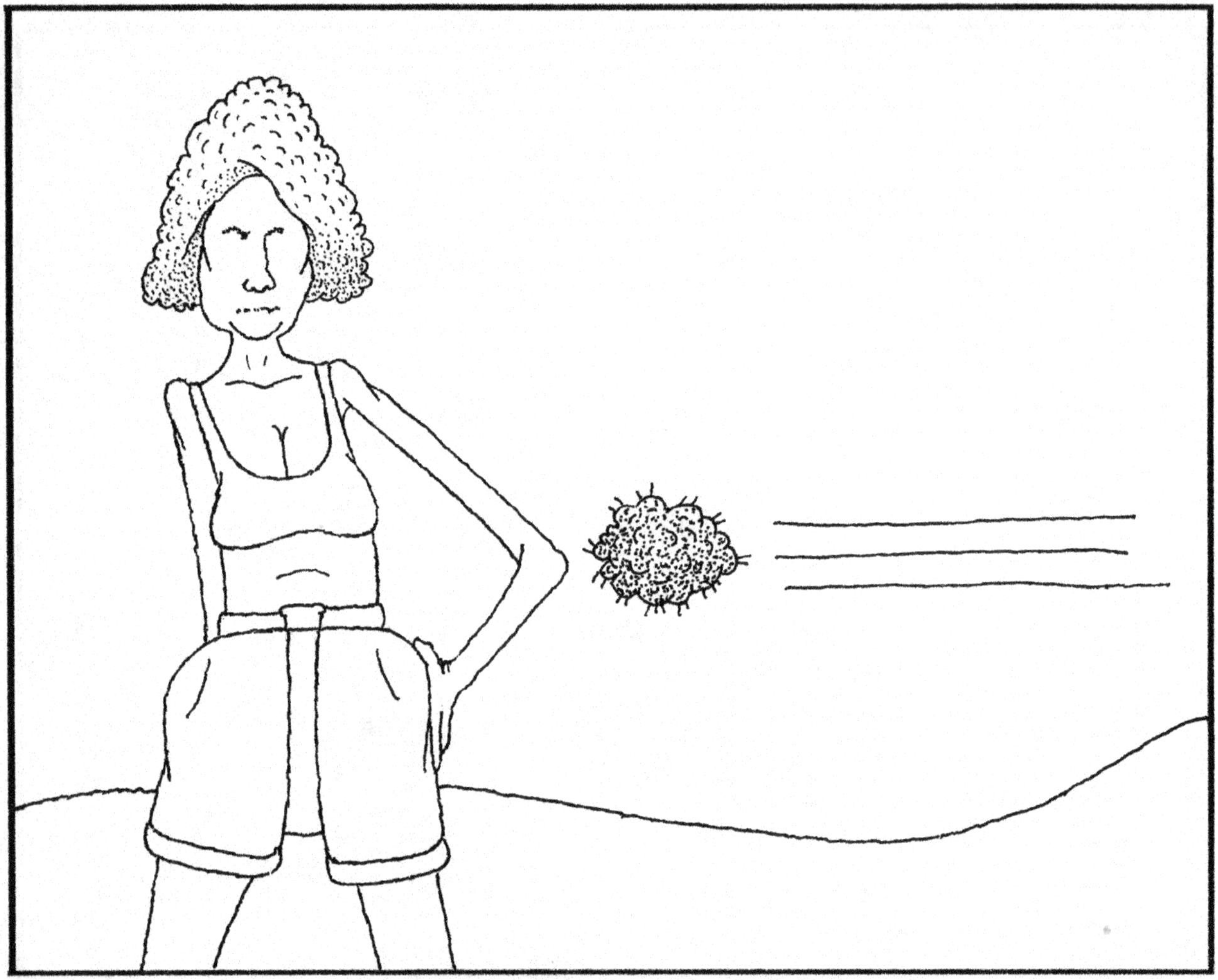

"AUNT JENNY'S ELBOW"

"DEVIL-MAY-CARE EGG WITH UNWITTING COMPANION"

"BALANCING BOBBY GOES TO THE RENAISSANCE FAIR DESPITE HIS FATHER'S BETTER JUDGEMENT"

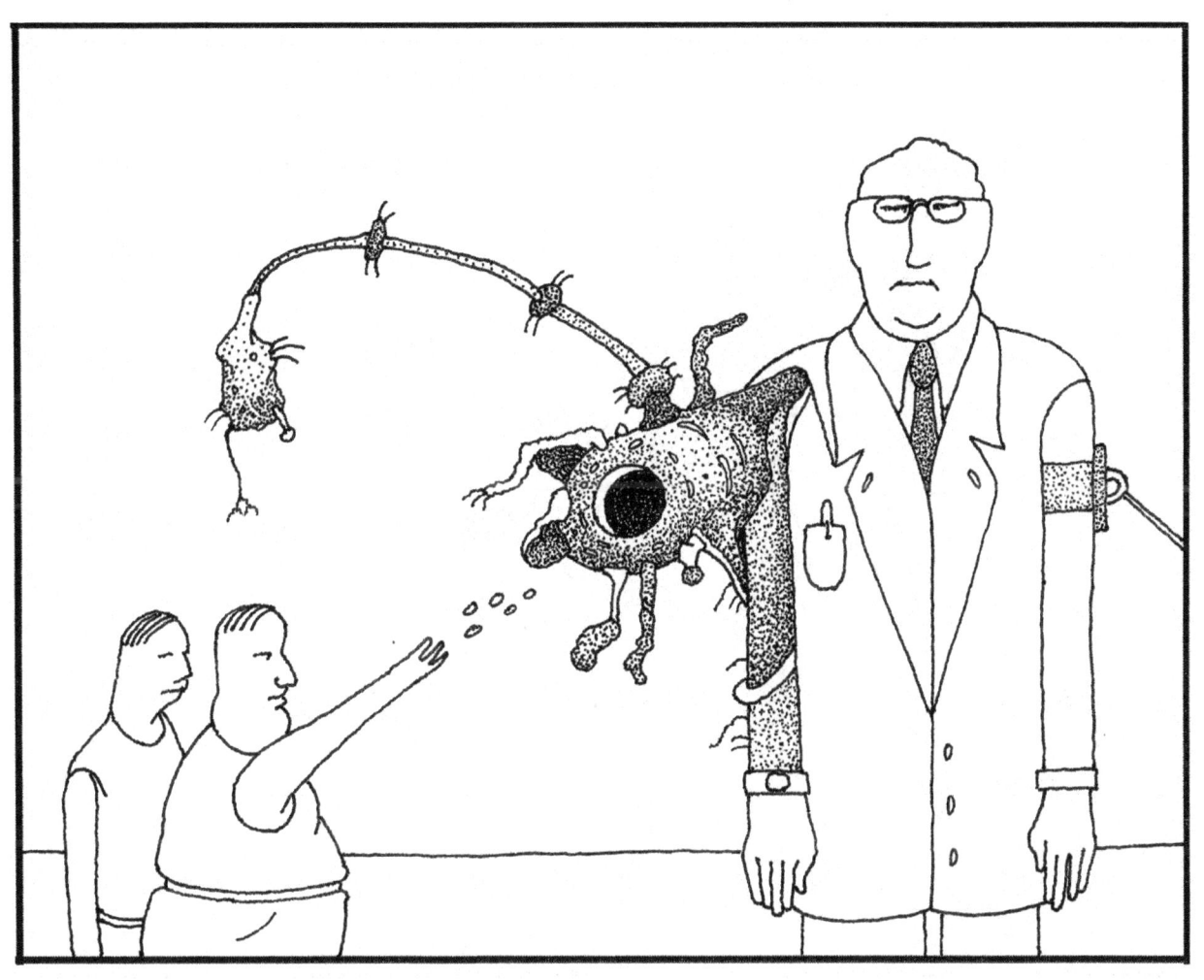

"DR. CARLSBAD OFTEN FORCED THE NEIGHBORHOOD KIDS TO TOSS HARD CANDY INTO HIS DEFORMITY"

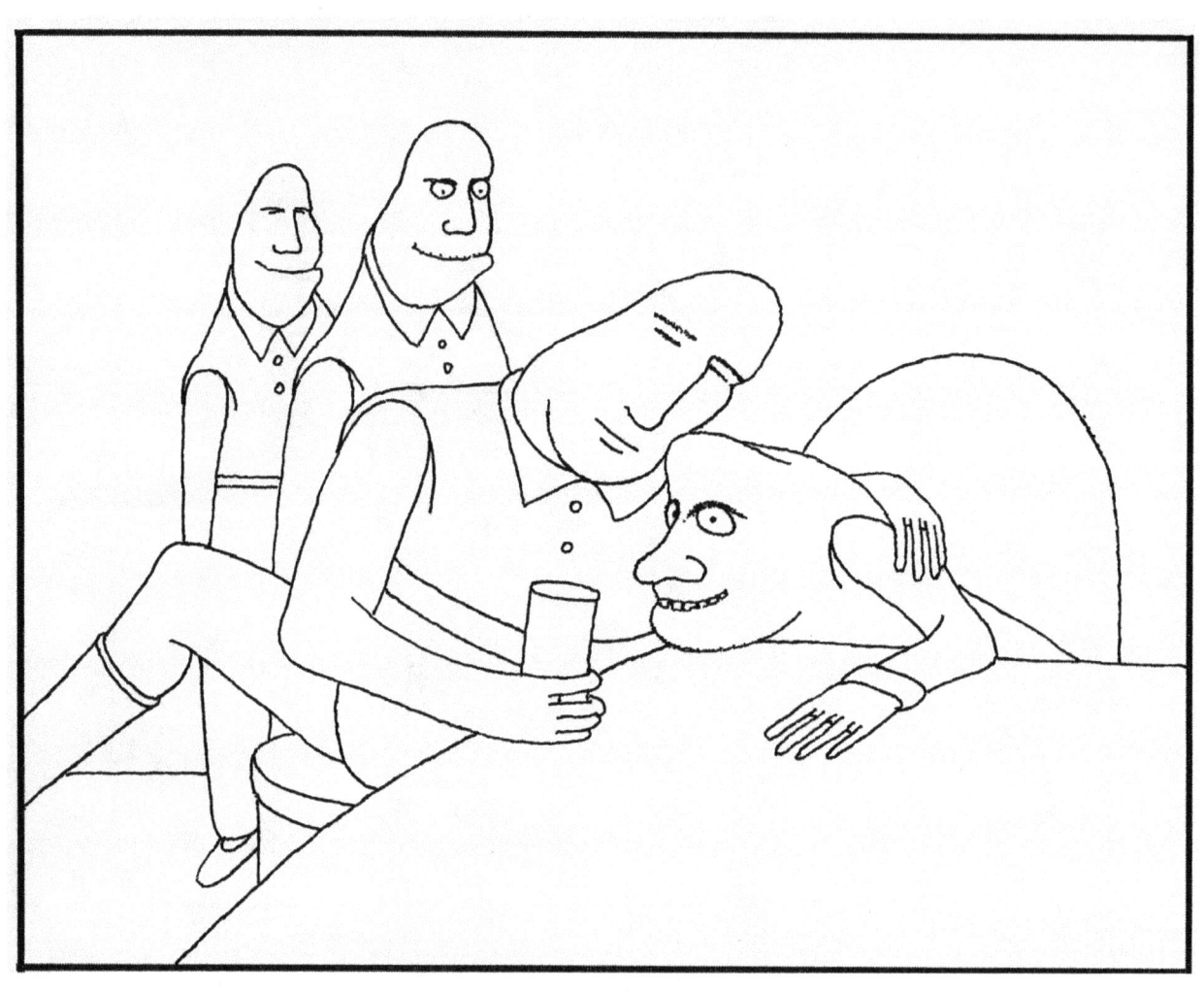

"LITTLE FREDDY'S FIRST GLASS OF SKIM MILK"

"GRANDPOP FINDS A BUNCH OF WEIRD CRAP ARRANGED ON HIS SLEEPING PLATFORM"

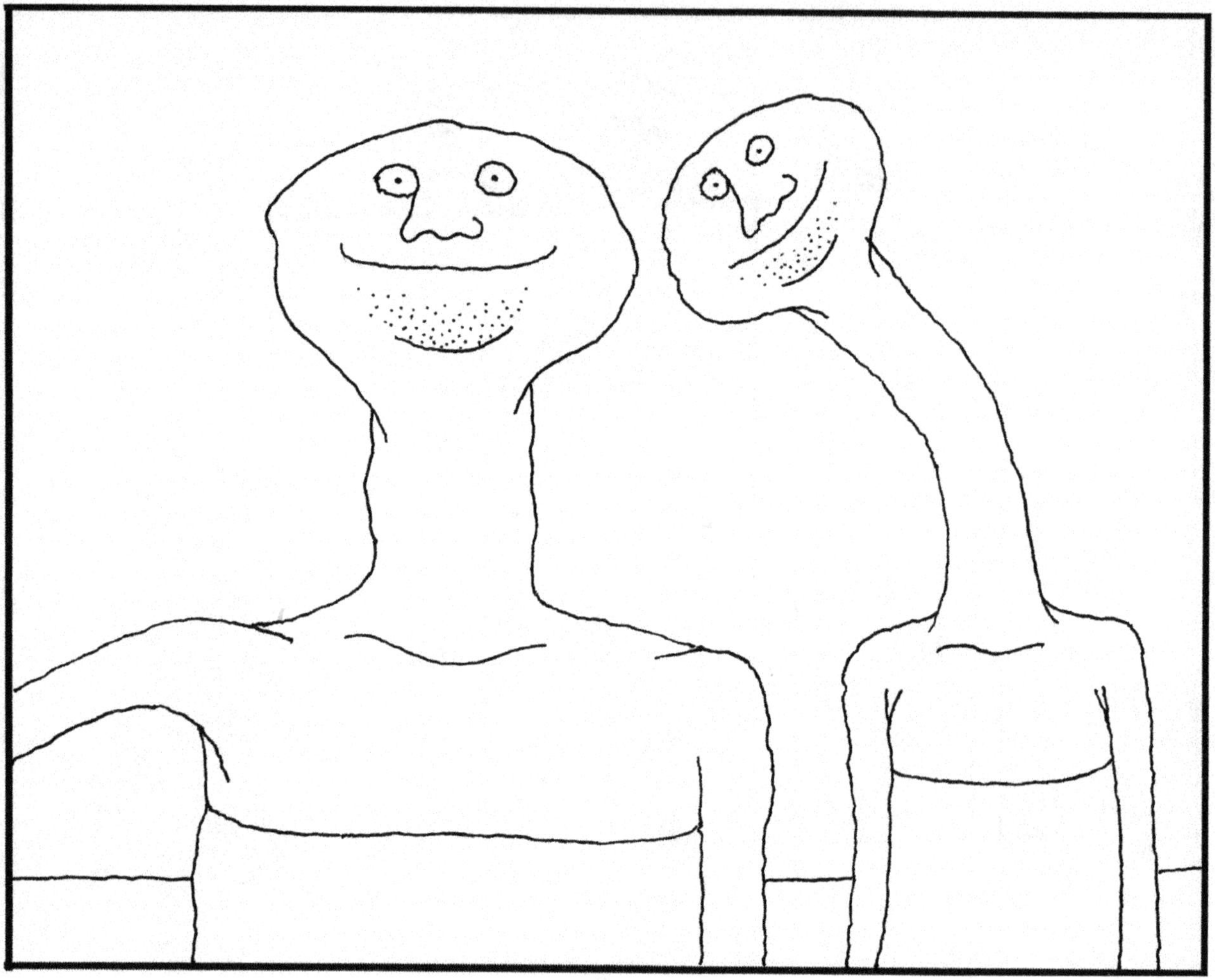

"SATISFIED ALIENS"

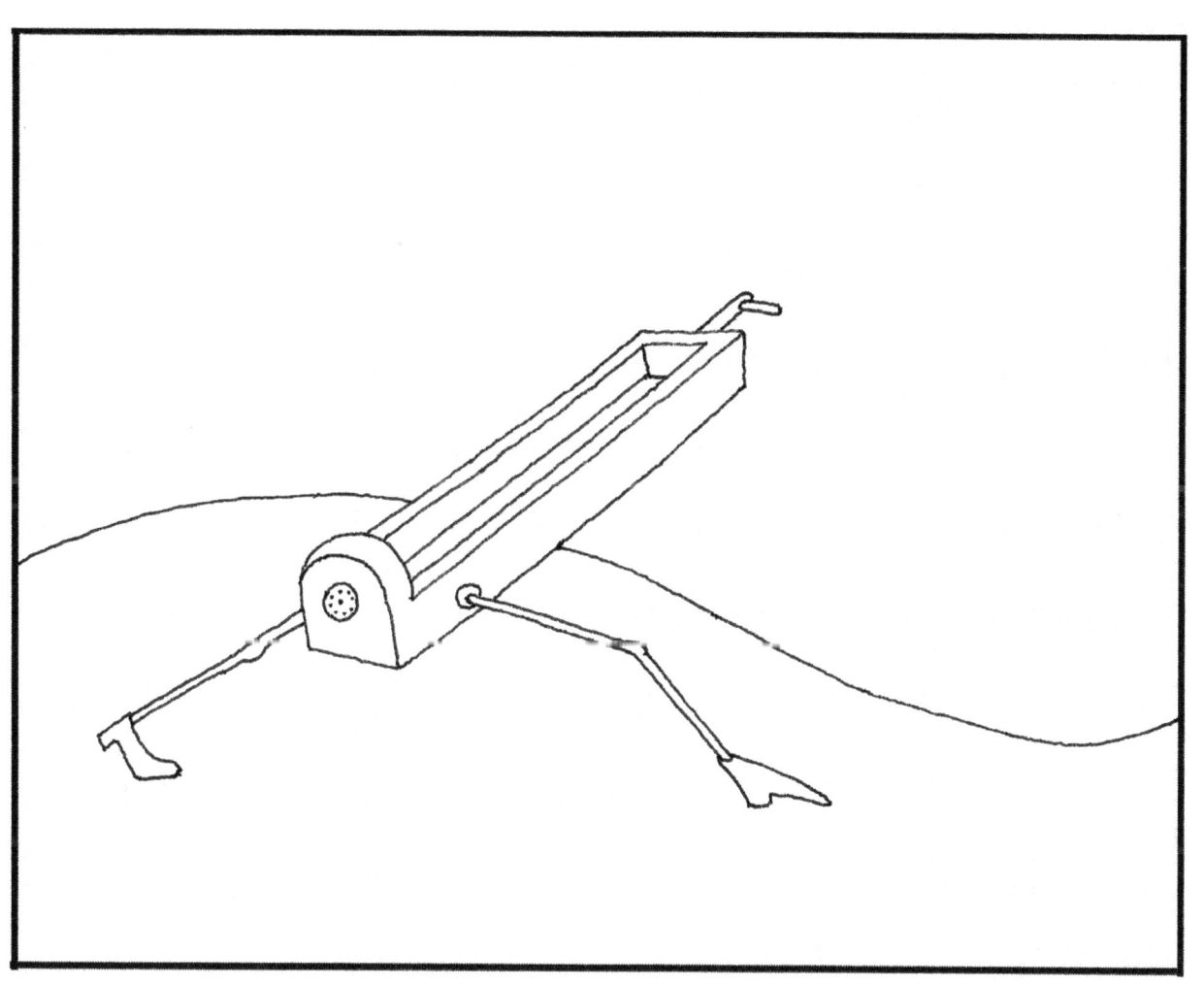

"OVERWORKED URINAL ON THE RUN"

"BIG WALLY POKES MR. HINYCAN WITH A TOOTHPICK"

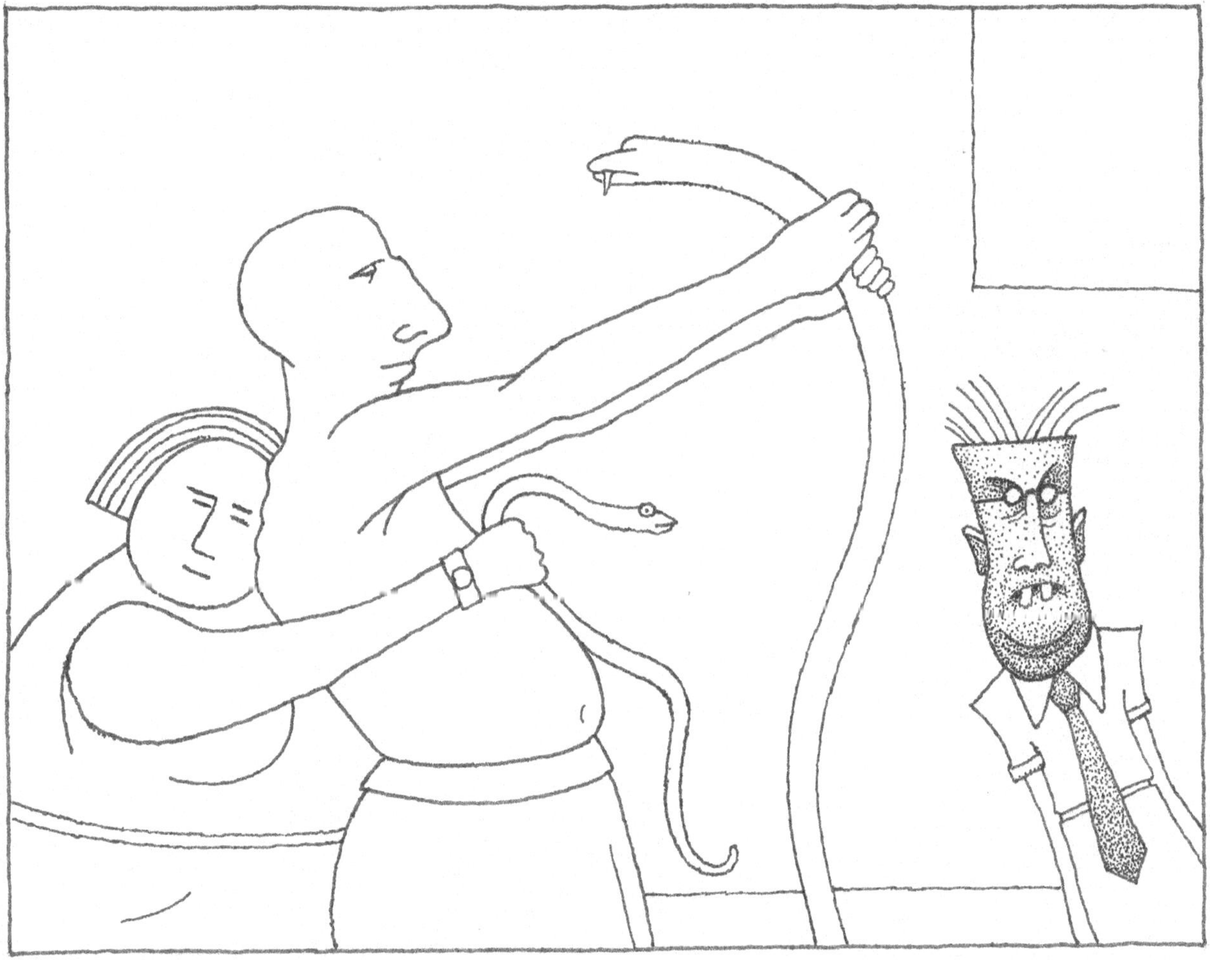

"DESPERATELY SEARCHING FOR A PUBLIC TOILET, ANGRY DAN ACCIDENTALLY FOUND HIMSELF IN SOME SORT OF RELIGIOUS SNAKE PIT"

"BETSY AND DAN SAT IN THE CORNER, QUIETLY DISINTEGRATING"

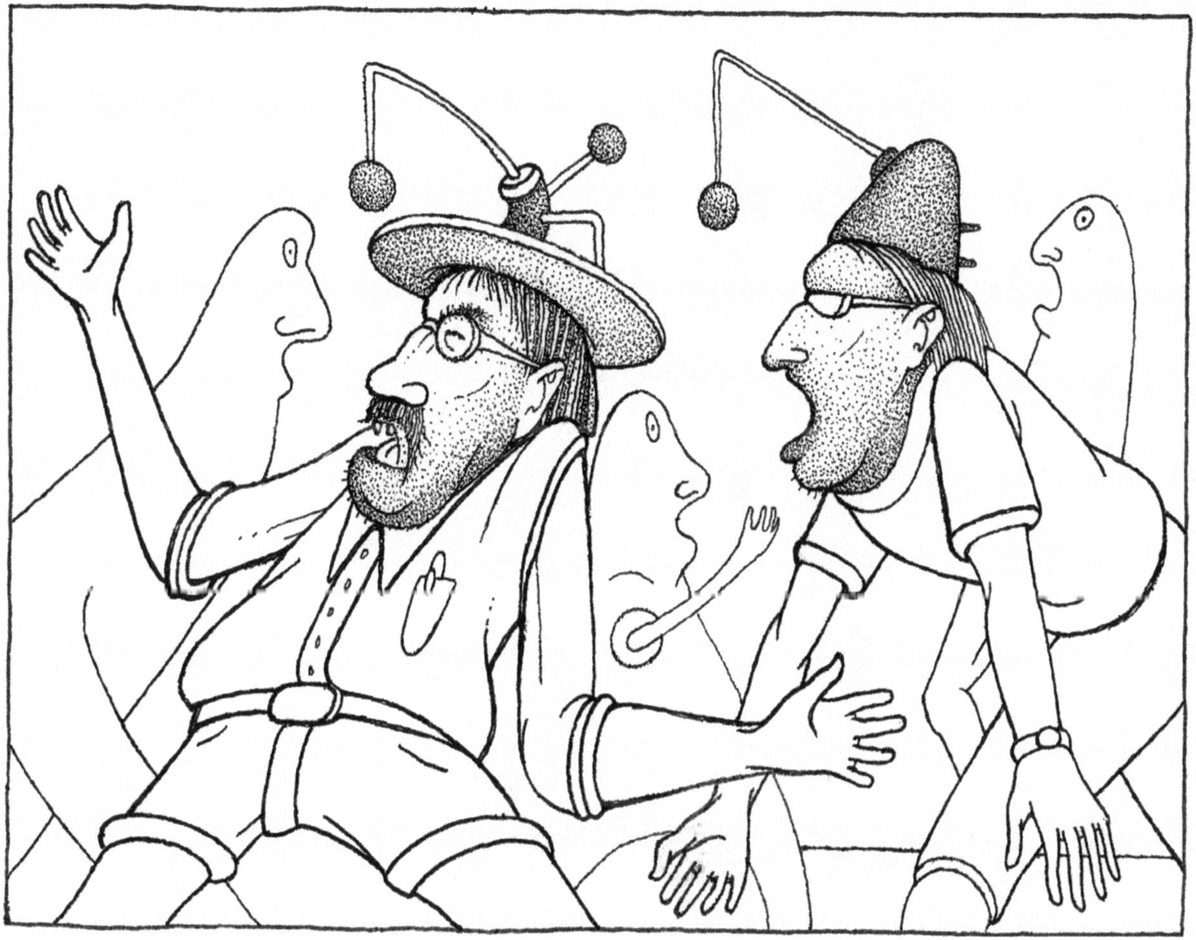

"DANCE CLASS IN HELL"

"OUT OF CONTROL UNICYCLIST"

"IN THE FUTURE IT WILL BE MANDATORY TO SHARE YOUR CHEESE WITH MUTANTS"

"DR. CRANSTON'S LITTLE BELL DID LITTLE TO IMPRESS THE HUMDOO PEOPLE"

"GOOD AND SIMPLE HENRY TRIES TO REASON WITH A MAN-BEAST KNOWN AS THE MIDNIGHT WORM"

"FILTHY ANDY PRESENTS MISS PHELPS WITH A BIG BOX OF ROTTEN CANDY"

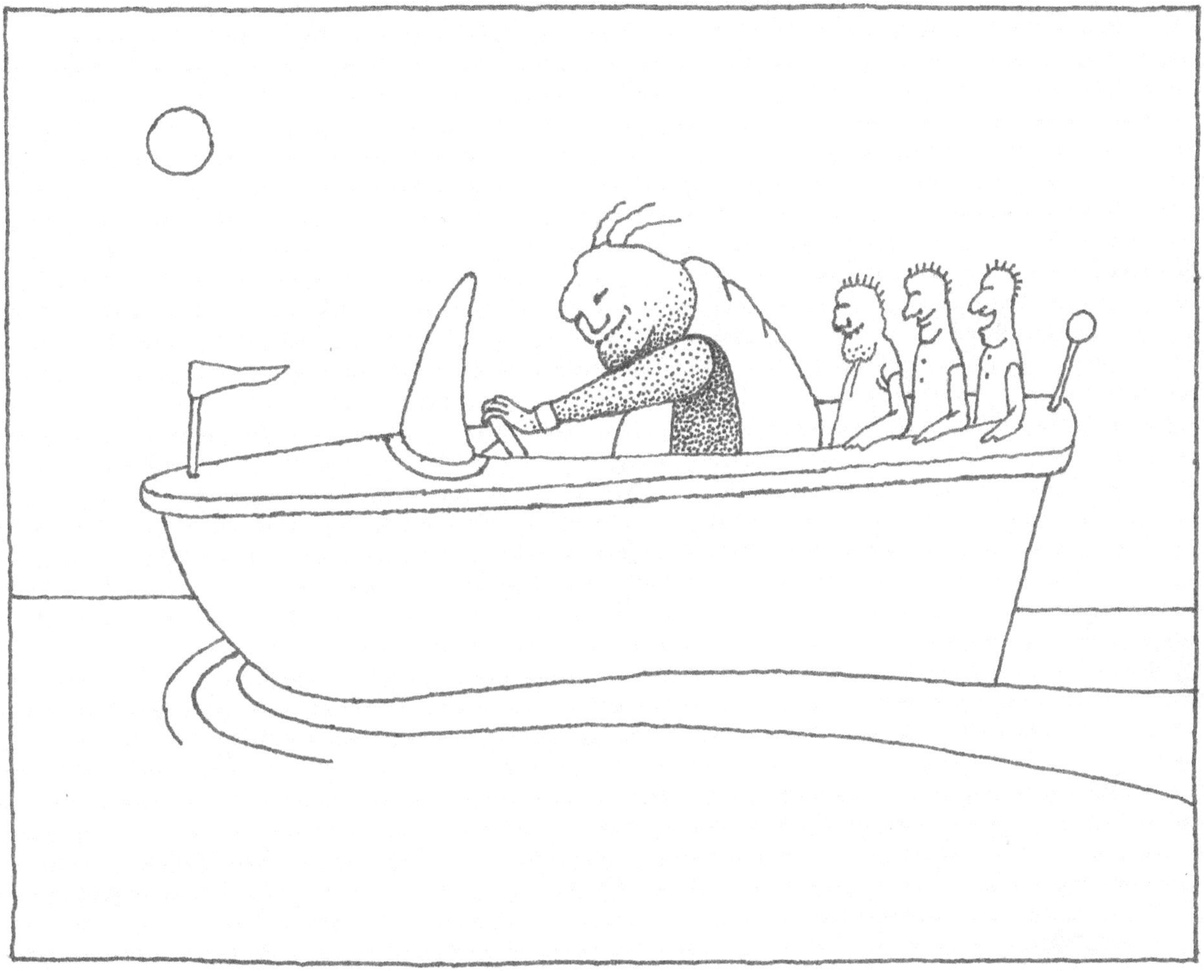

"LAKESIDE PLEASURES"

"FIRST DISADVANTAGED FAMILY BLASTED INTO OUTER SPACE"

"JUST BEFORE THE GATES OF HEAVEN"

"SHERIFF BEASTHORN SUSPECTS THAT HENRY'S MUFFIN WAS STOLEN"

"LOCAL GENIUS AND HIS DEVICE"

"FORTY SECONDS INTO HIS FIRST SONG, THE AUDIENCE ATTACKED LITTLE JIMMY MCMANUS, DESTROYING HIS PROPS AND BURNING HIS WIG"

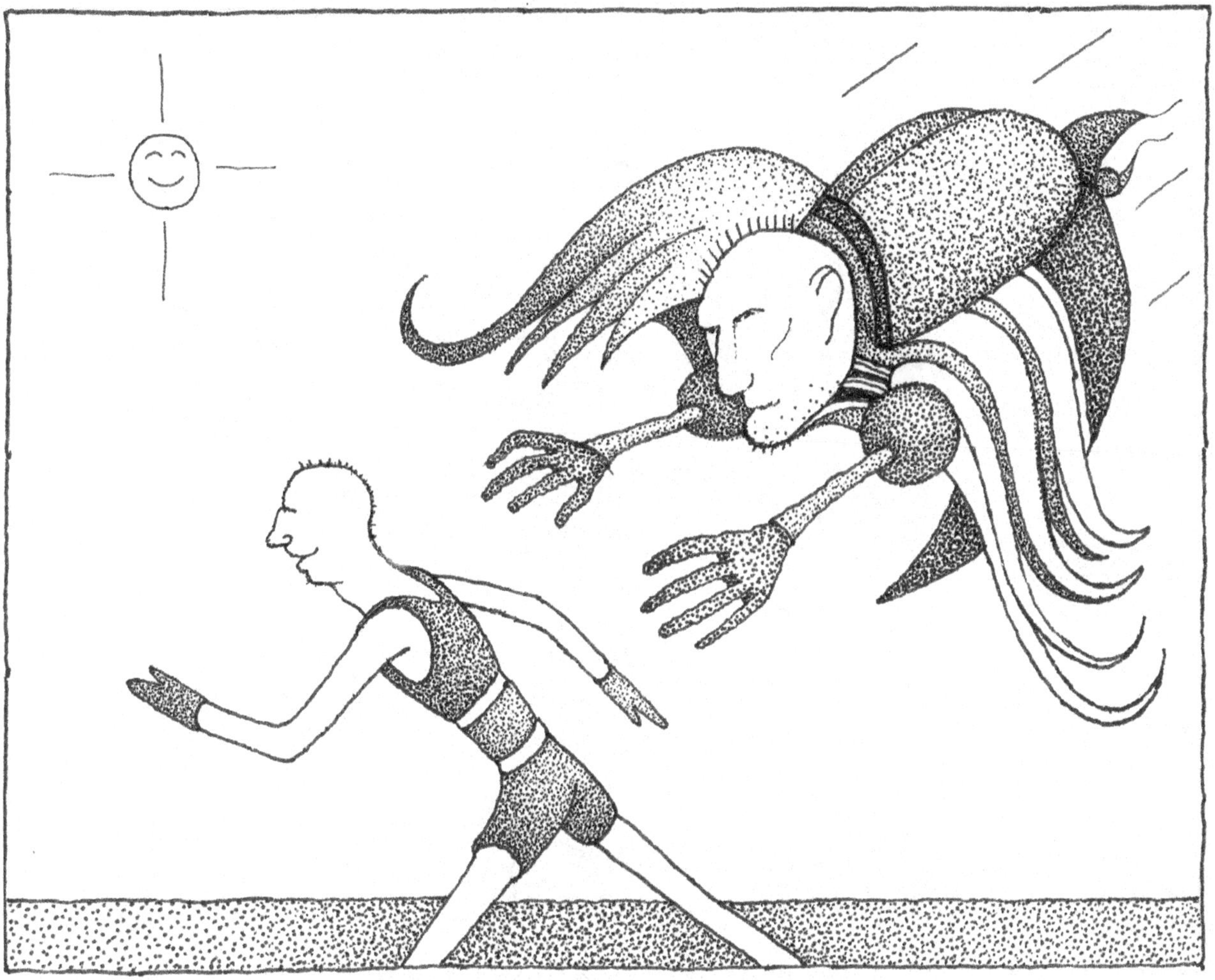

"GOOD DAY BAD DAY"

"IT WAS ALL BUTCH HARTIGAN COULD DO TO KEEP FROM STRANGLING FLIMSY JIMMY"

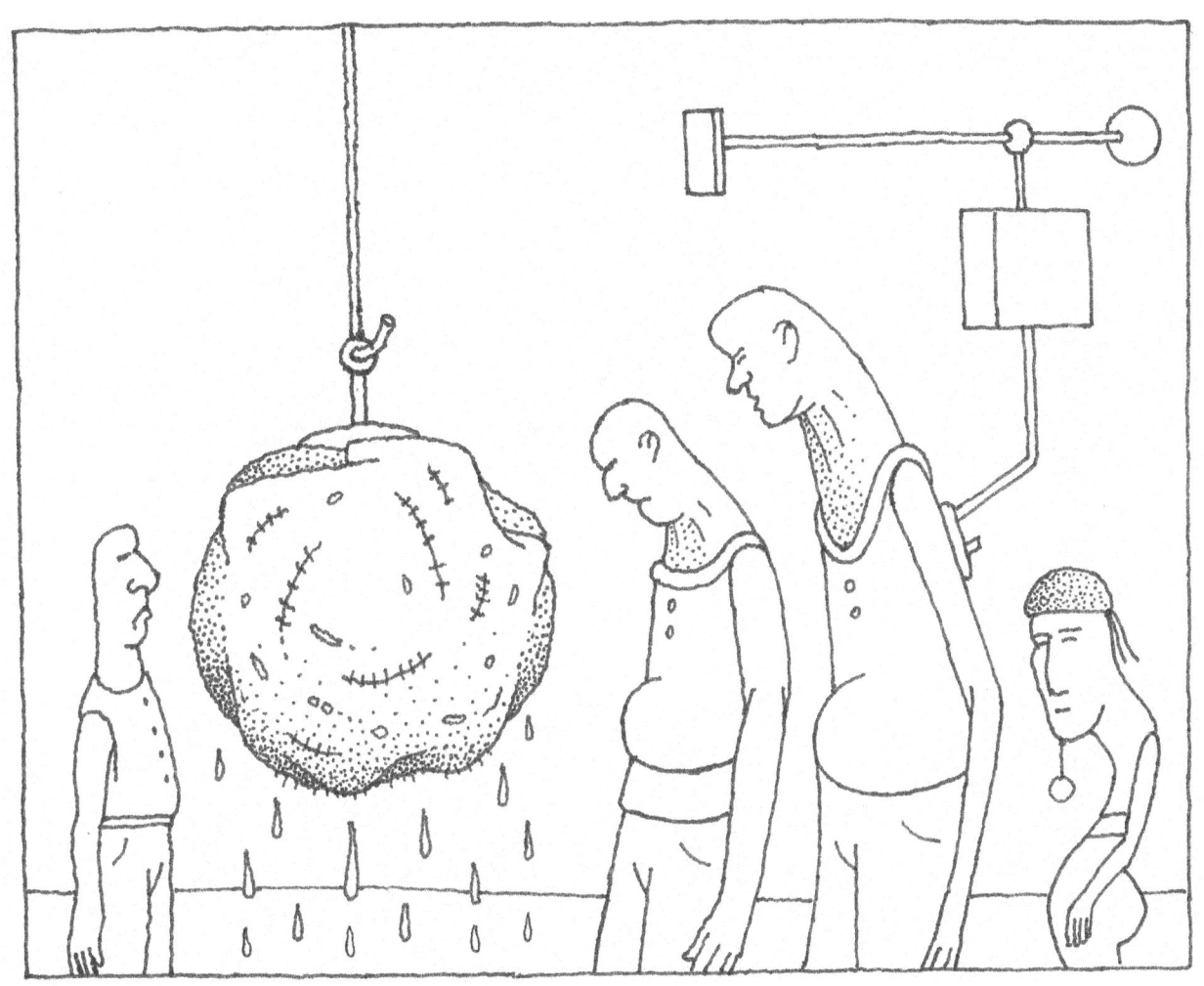

"BACKYARD ENIGMA"

"BOWLING BALL WITH VANILLA PUDDING"

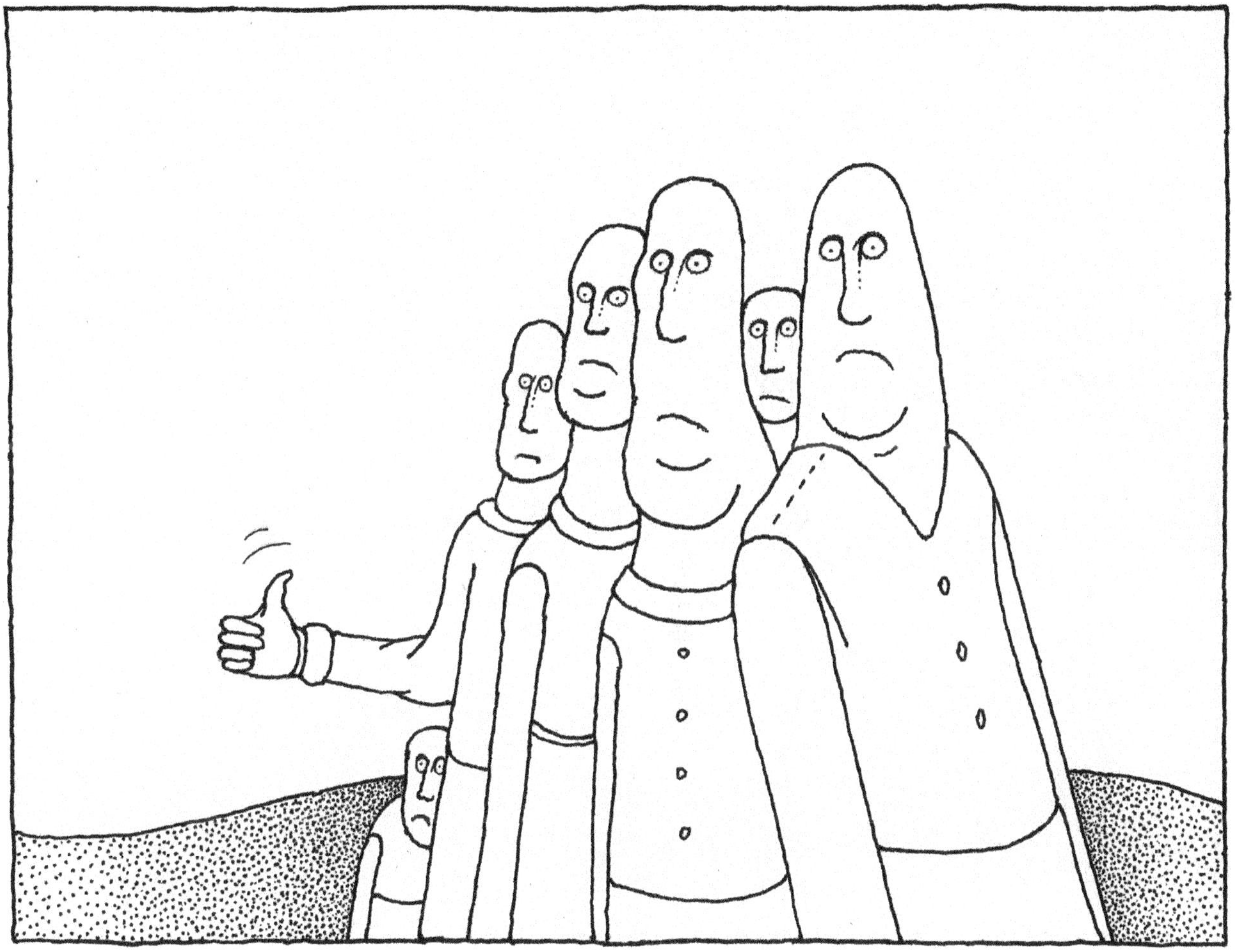

"DEMENTED HITCHHIKERS"

"NANCY LIKED TO HOVER OVER THE DINING TABLE, SILENTLY BREAKING VAST AMOUNTS OF WIND"

"SHE DIDN'T KNOW WHO THEY WERE, OR WHAT THEY WANTED, BUT THEY WERE ALWAYS THERE"

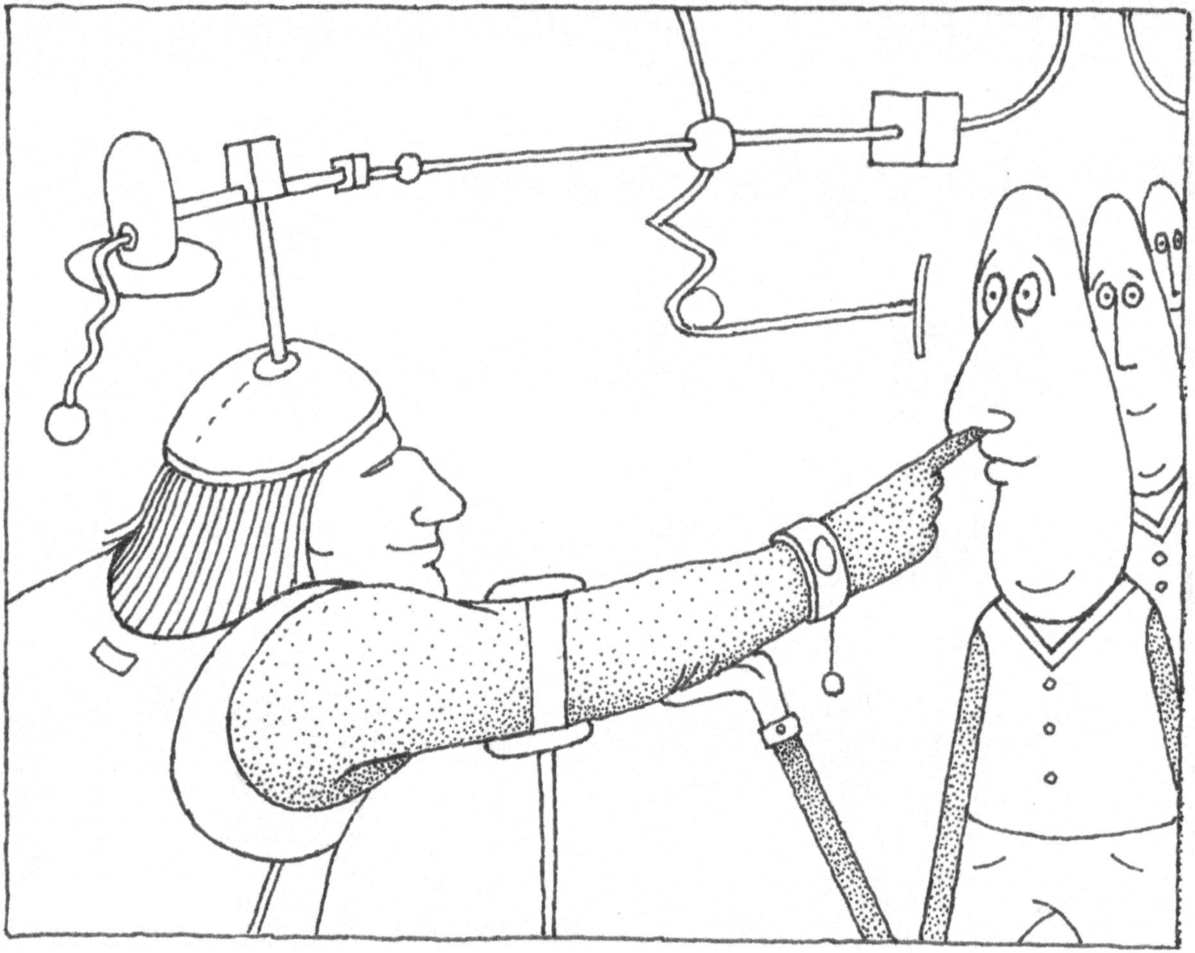

"NASAL SHENANIGANS"

"SELF-PROCLAIMED GURUS PANTOMIMING THE FACTS OF LIFE FOR FILTHY WILLIAM"

"MIRACLE CURES THROUGH ESSENCE OF TOENAIL"

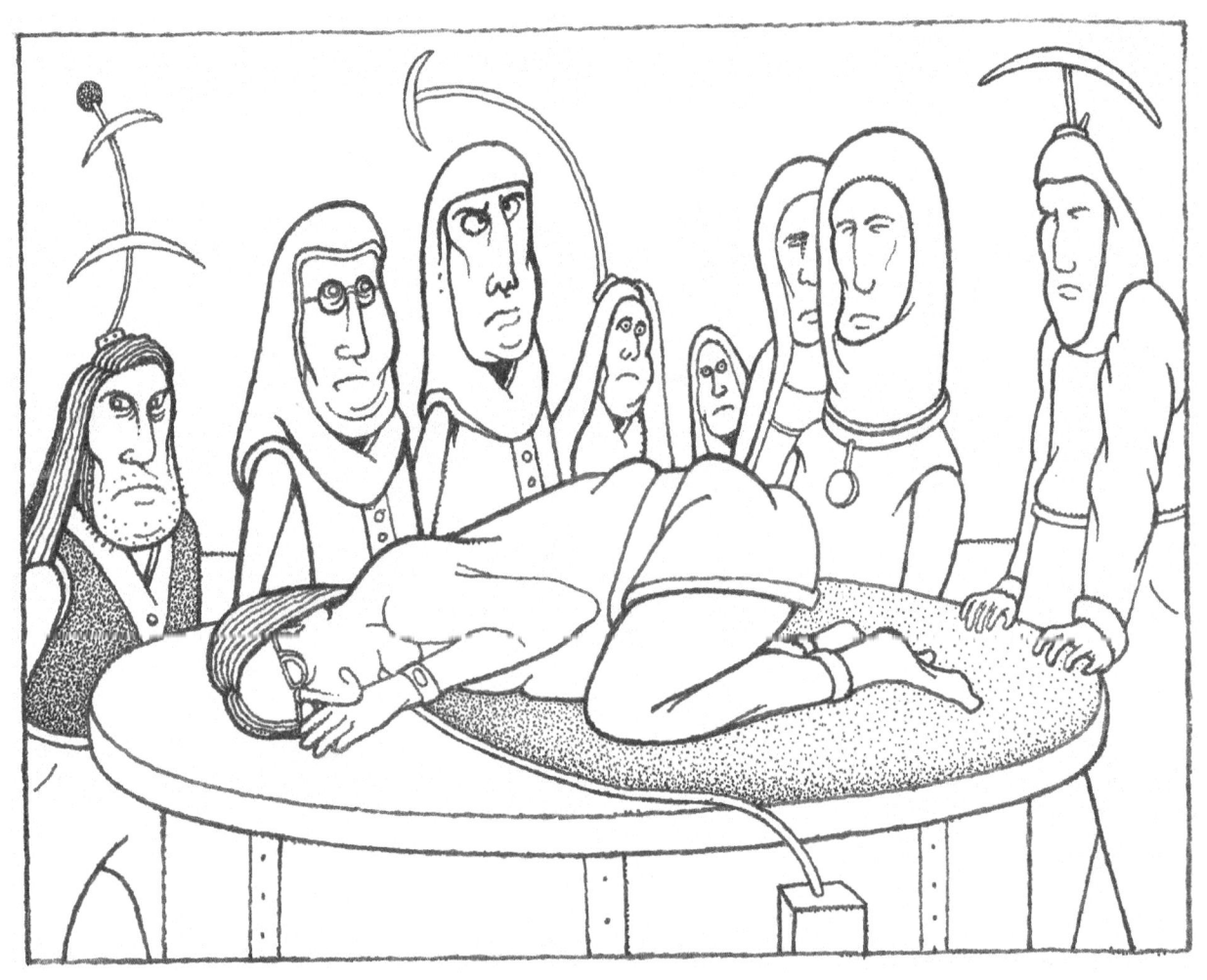

"WHEN YOU'VE FINALLY DISAPPOINTED EVERYONE, THERE'S ALWAYS THE FETAL POSITION"

"NASTY HUMAN FLY WITH MAGNIFICENT PIECE OF CHEESECAKE"

"TRUE LOVE KNOWS NO BOUNDARIES"

"NEVER PUT A RAT ON A PEDESTAL"

"SKETCHY INDIVIDUAL PURSUING THE SPHERE OF CONTENTMENT"

"TWENTY SECONDS BEFORE THE BIG BANG"

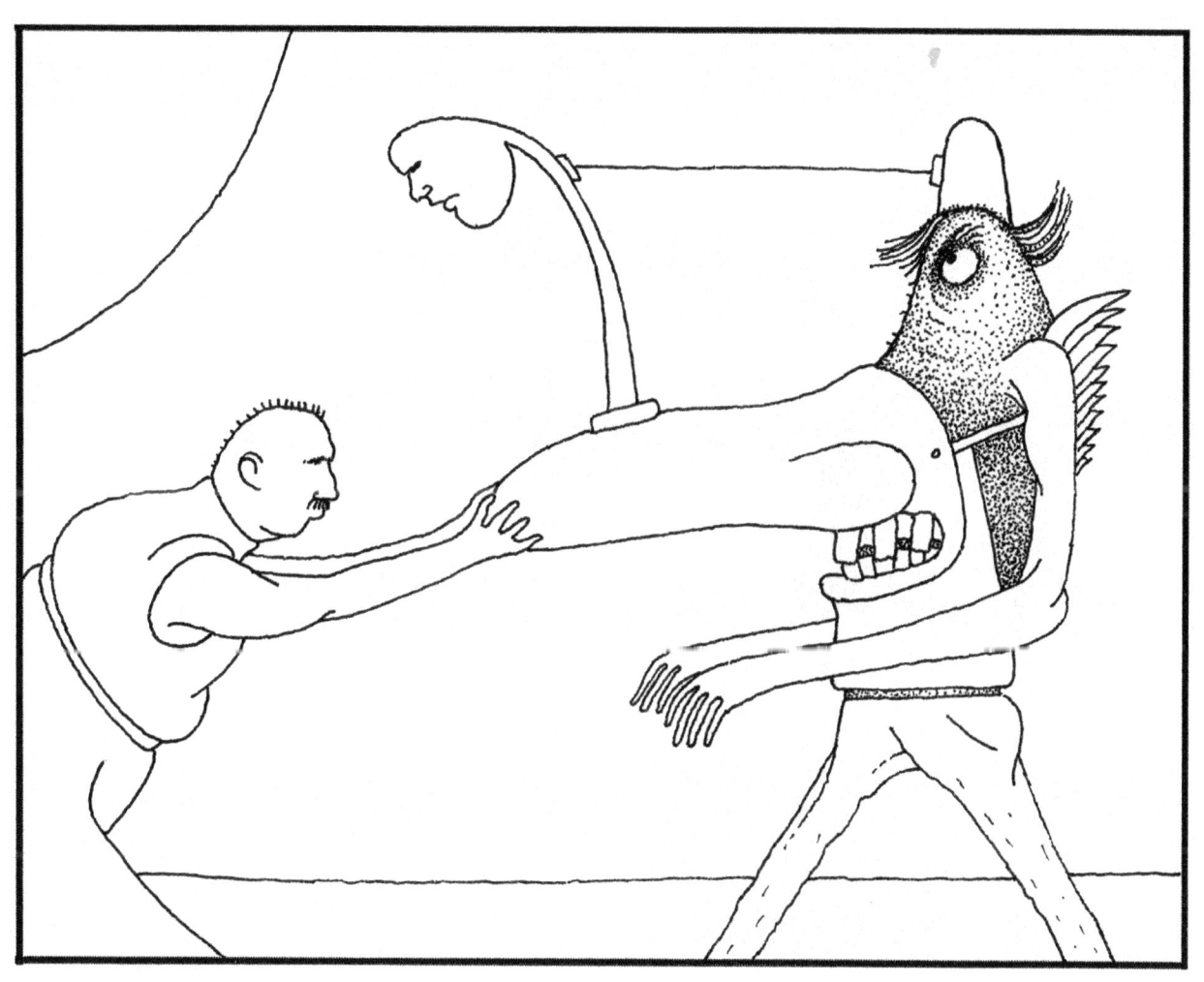

"TAMING THE LEGENDARY VERSHKLABITER BEAST"

"WEIRD WALKIN' STALKER ESCAPING THE LAW"

"TEACHING MRS. MUSSMAN TO DANCE"

"TIMMY FINDS TWO OTHER TIMMYS LIVING IN HIS SOCK DRAWER"

"THE WILKERSON BROTHERS ALWAYS HAD SOMETHIN' SPECIAL GOIN' ON"

"FATHER KUROWSKI FINALLY GETS HIS CHANCE TO HIT THE PANIC BUTTON"

"HOSTILE SPHEREOIDS SHARING A LATTE"

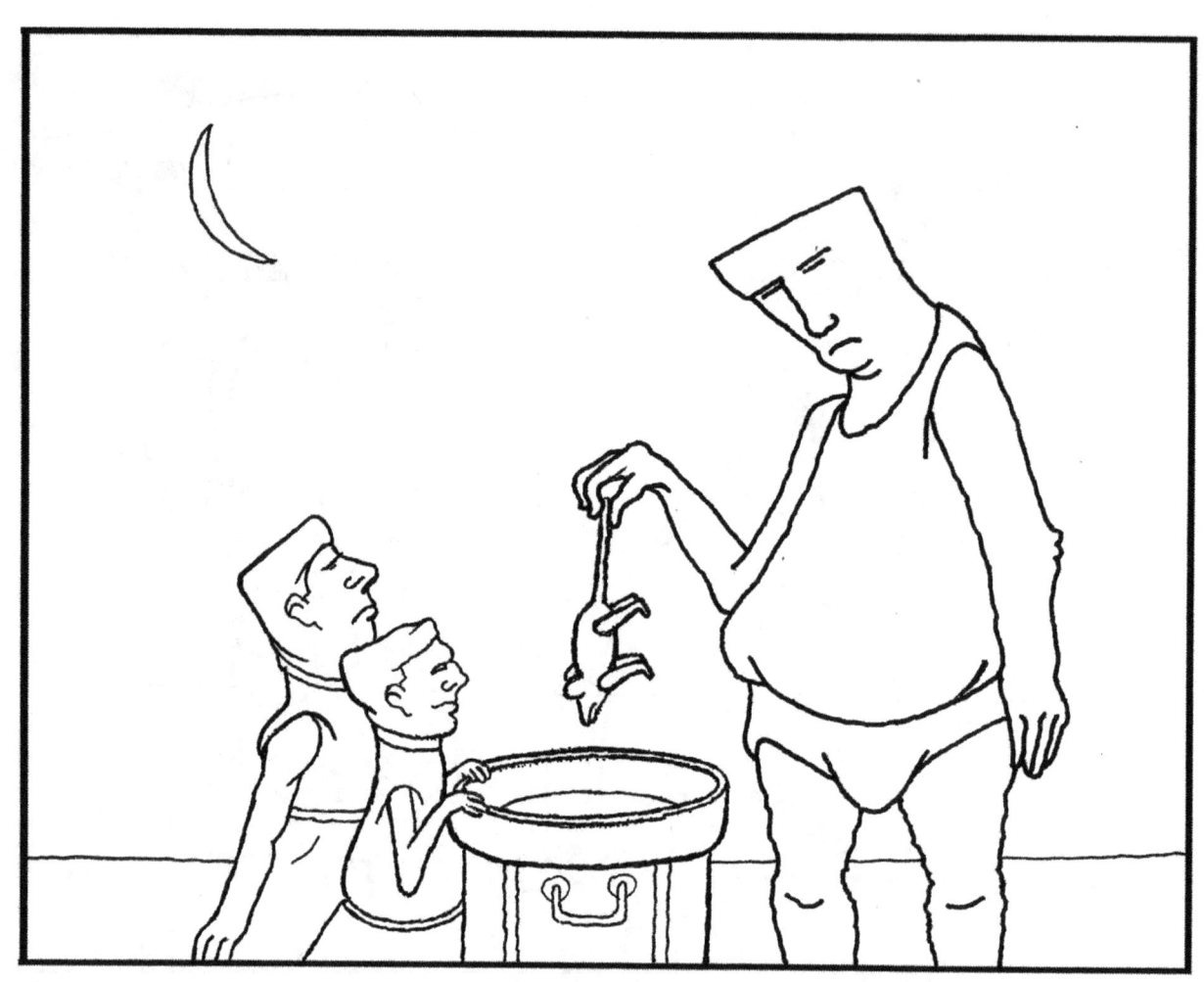
"THROWING OUT A RAT"

"EVEN DEAD TREES HATED POOR LITTLE NANCY SPURLINGER"

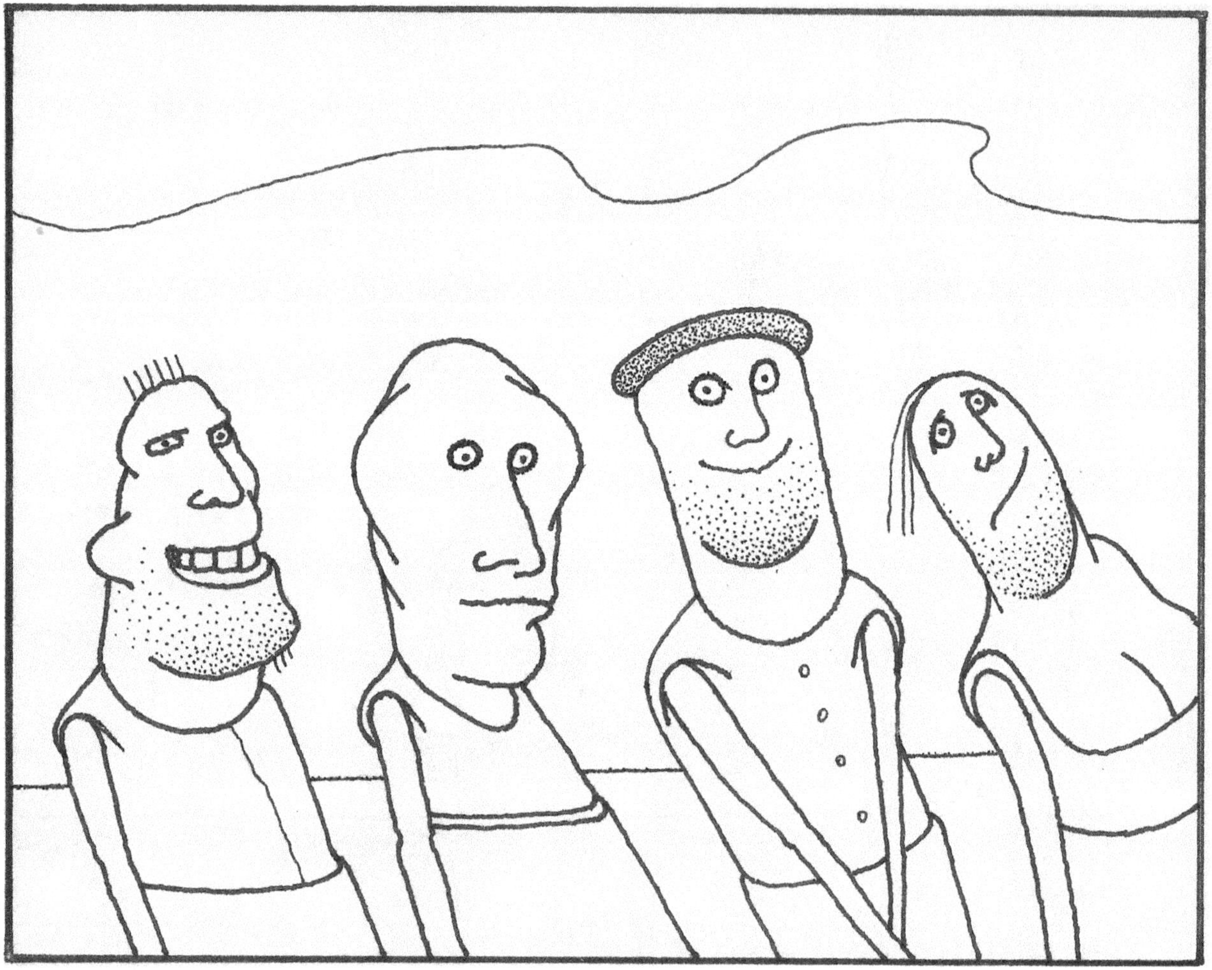

“HOPEFUL CONTESTANTS”

"SAINT VAN DOOKAS COMFORTS THE EGG MAN"

"SCREWED-UP LAWN ORNAMENTS"

"MR. PEEBLES AND MR. VAN HORST, ATTORNEYS AT LAW"

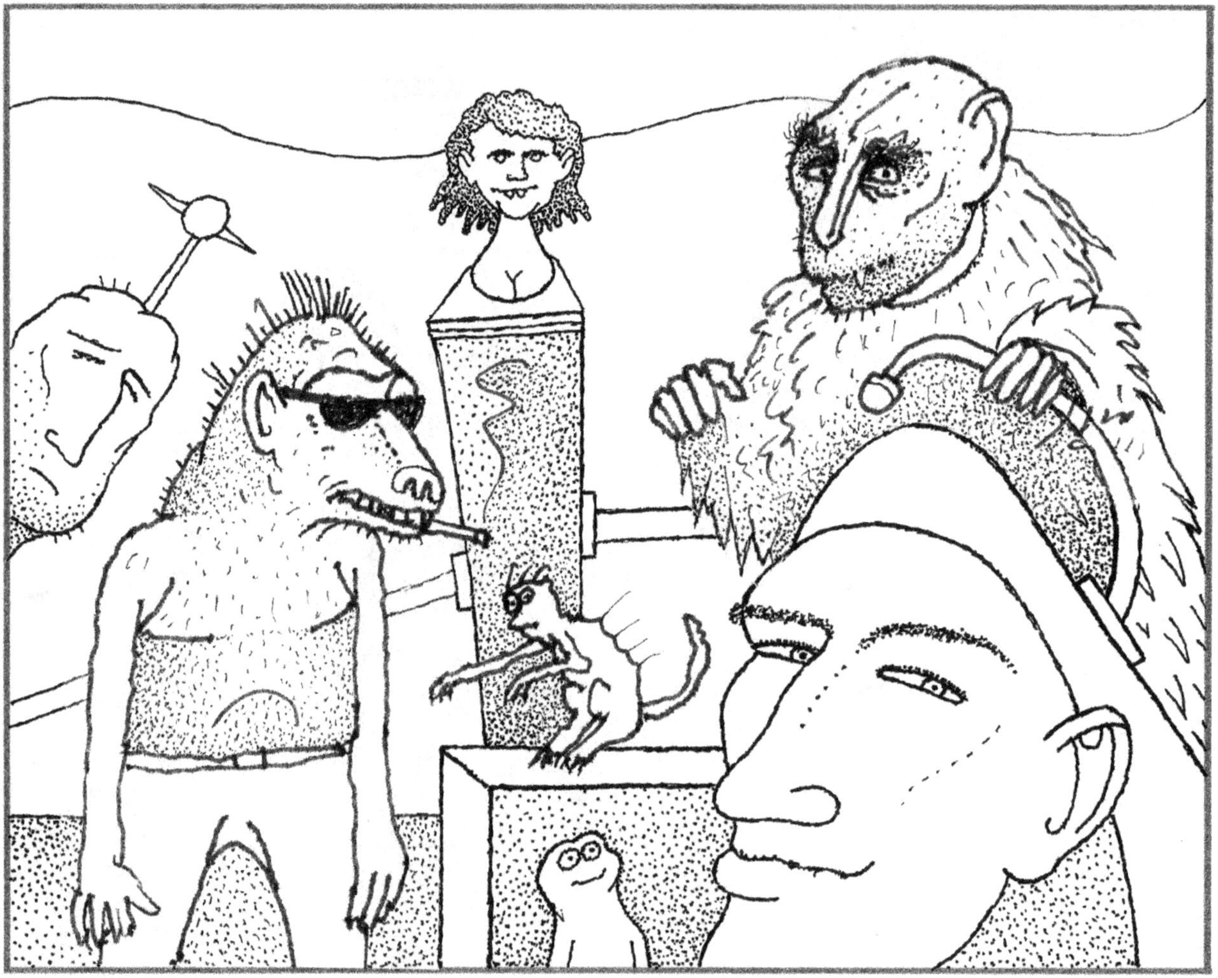

"CLASS REUNION"

"NICE DAY FOR A WALK IN THE PARK"

"DOWN AT THE OLD MASSIVE AND HAIRY BOOGER EXCHANGE"

"MILDLY DISTURBING SCENARIO WITH TINY DANCER"

"BRINGING AN EGG TO A BOIL"

"REVOLTING RABBIT FAMILY WITH AXE MURDERER"

"THE FIRST AND LAST JOURNEY OF TRUTH SEEKERS ANONYMOUS"

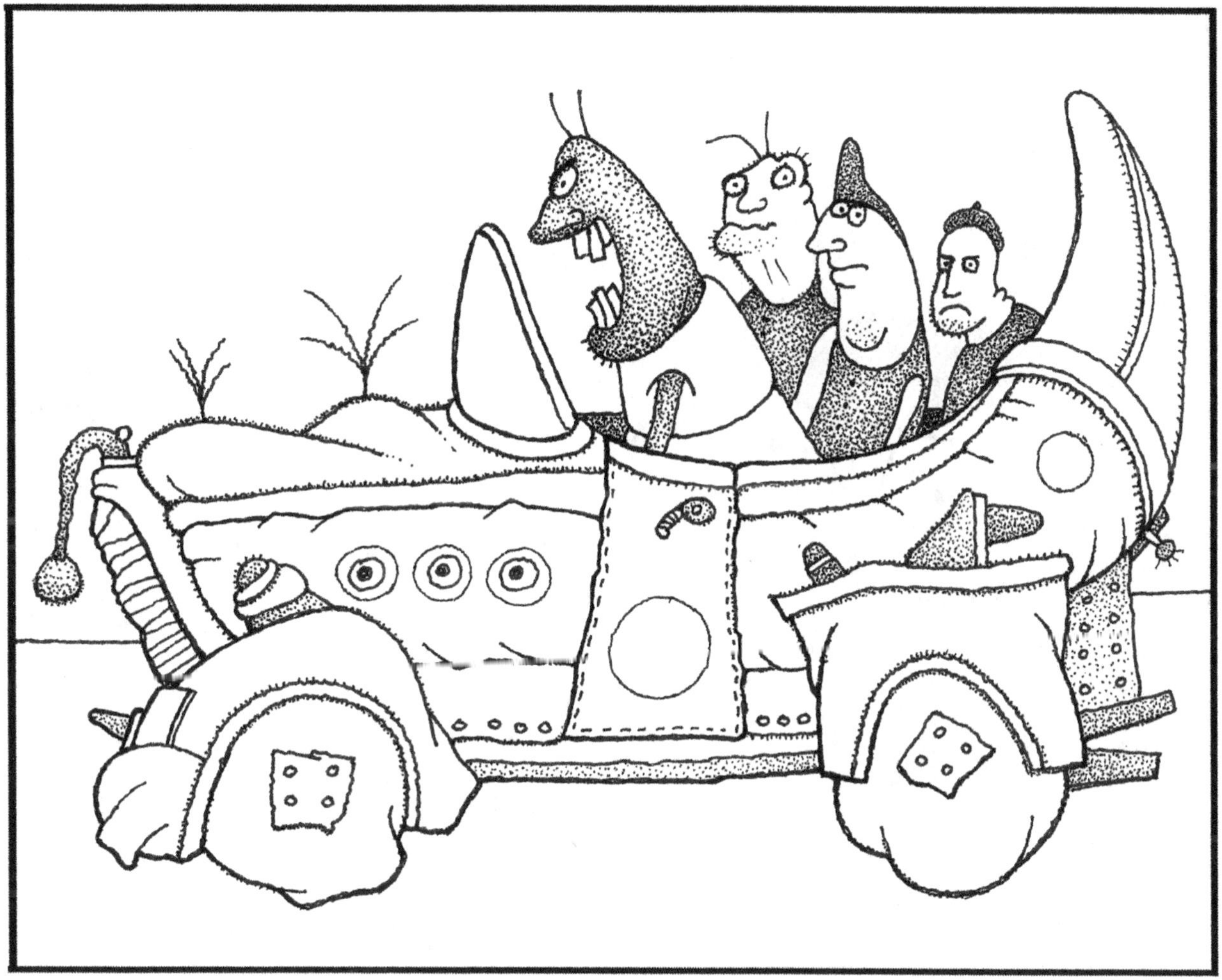

"OUT OF GAS"

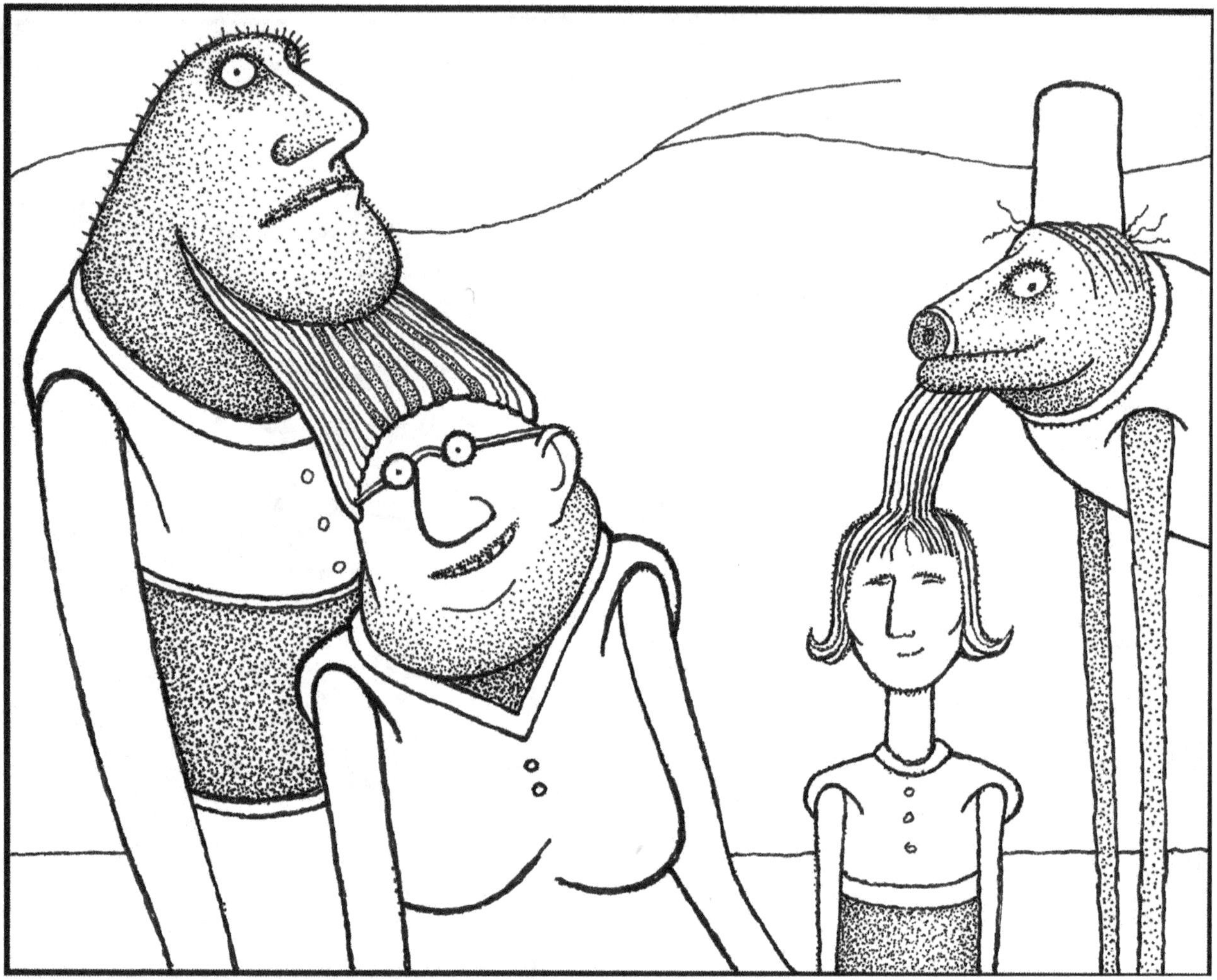

"BEARD-WIG COMBOS"

"REALLY WEIRD BIRTHDAY PARTY"

"CAPTAIN JACK FLANNIGAN (USN RETIRED) DETONATES A HOMEMADE STINK BOMB"

DENNIS CORRIGAN

Dennis Corrigan was born in 1944 in Lakewood, New Jersey, and raised with his four brothers in Toms River, New Jersey. He attended Philadelphia College of Art where he received a BFA in Illustration in 1966, then, after a three-year stint in the Navy, an MFA in Painting from Tyler School of Art, Temple University in 1972.

During the 1970s Corrigan received worldwide recognition for his intricate pencil renderings of displaced pop political figures in congested, flattened nineteenth century inspired interiors. Such notable publishers as Random House in NYC, and *Politiks Magazine* commissioned him for the use of such images. The images, with titles such as *Queen Victoria Troubled by Flies* and *President Nixon Hiding in a Small Town*, were inspired in part by his love for Victorian architecture, and the fourteen room Italianate mansion in Hawley, PA where he resided with his first wife and daughters, Sara and Rebecca. It was during this time that Corrigan also produced two illustrated adult storybooks. *The Spotter* is the story of a Civil Air Patrol volunteer, who, out of boredom and opportunity, is compelled to take up voyeurism. *The Amusement Park* is a thinly veiled symbolic account of his impending divorce.

In 1980, Corrigan married his second wife, Donna, also an artist, who inspired him to experiment with oil painting. Using an unconventional palette of oranges, greens and violets, and their intermixtures, he produced a series of dark and moody surreal landscapes, which served as backdrops for a cast of lonely and mysterious characters. Though these characters are no one in particular, we immediately recognize them as representatives of the human condition in raw form. The paintings, with titles like *Red Madonna*, *Sly Cat at Sunset* and *Going Home*, are among Corrigan's more poignant, non-humorous works. It is not until the late 1980s that Corrigan reduces his characters to a more simplified form, and introduces a humorous literary component to his work. The titles of these paintings, such as *Nuts Looking for Squirrels*, *Three Men Holding a Grudge*, and *Man with a Smirk on His Face*, further illuminate the visual pun that was the inspiration for the piece.

The 1990s found Dennis Corrigan venturing into the third dimension. A confirmed hoarder of "interesting shapes" and discarded materials, Corrigan was now combining and arranging disparate elements to create surreal objects. The richly adorned furniture-like pieces appear at first to have a particular function, but upon closer inspection, it becomes apparent that the stationary hinges, trap doors and staging devices are intended to merely entertain. These sculptures are of two separate varieties: purely objective, as with Portable Confessional and Fetish Object, and pictorial, as with Man Being Chased by a Furball.

Corrigan's latest works in video and humor are an amalgam of his previous interests with the addition of motion and sound. The most compelling expression of Dennis' life is a documentary film entitled "Corrigan vs. Corrigan", wherein he is shown as a very humourous, extroverted introvert, seeking a wider audience for his endless and increasing flood of uniquely creative thoughts, expressed in drawings, paintings, sculpture, assemblage, and video.

Dennis Corrigan is Assistant Professor of Art at Marywood University in Scranton, PA.

—*Donna Pacinelli Corrigan*

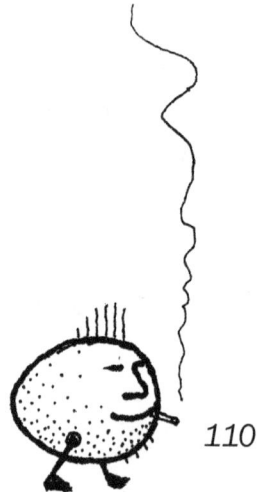

For more information about Dennis Corrigan and TRUE LOVE KNOWS NO BOUNDARIES contact lee@avventurapress.com.

Title	Page
A Hole Full of Happiness	16
A Huge and Hideous Floating Butt Bedevils Young Saint Nick	28
After Mom Became Dad, We Lived on Nothing But Marshmallows and Croutons	33
An Abnormal Primate Tries to Purchase Shy Benjamin's Special Hat	40
Aunt Jenny's Elbow	46
Backyard Enigma	71
Balancing Bobby Goes to The Renaissance Fair Despite His Father's Better Judgement	48
Beard-Wig Combos	106
Betsy and Dan Sat in The Corner, Quietly Disintegrating	56
Big Wally Pokes Mr. Hinycan with a Toothpick	54
Bowling Ball with Vanilla Pudding	72
Branch Managers	17
Bringing an Egg to a Boil	102
Bullwhip Surprise	20
Captain Jack Flannigan (USN Retired) Detonates a Homemade Stink Bomb	110
Class Reunion	98
Clumsy Woman, with Roving Eye, Bowling in the Desert	11
Cube-Headed Lunatic Holding Up a Lemonade Stand	36
Dad Taught Himself to Steer the Family Sedan with His Enormous, Sticky Tongue	18
Dance Class in Hell	57
Demented Hitchhikers	73
Desperately Searching for a Public Toilet, Angry Dan…	55
Devil-May-Care Egg with Unwitting Companion	47
Dirty Albert Licks the Back of Frank's Head Despite Mr. Fong's Disapproval	41
Down at the Old Massive and Hairy Booger Exchange	100
Dr. Carlsbad Often Forced the Neighborhood Kids to Toss Hard Candy into His Deformity	49
Dr. Cranston's Little Bell Did Little to Impress the Humdoo People	60
Even Dead Trees Hated Poor Little Nancy Spurlinger	93
Fat Guys with Propellors, Laughing at a Stick of Butter	19
Father Kurowski Finally Gets His Chance to Hit the Panic Button	90
Filthy Andy Presents Miss Phelps with a Big Box of Rotten Candy	62
First Disadvantaged Family Blasted into Outer Space	64
Forty Seconds into His First Song, the Audience Attacked Little Jimmy Mc Manus…	68
Fresh from the Warm Embrace of an Antique Toilet, Senator Blanchard…	44
Friendly Neighbor, Just Passing By	10
God Bless Toilet Power	22
Good and Simple Henry Tries to Reason with a Man-Beast Known as the Midnight Worm	61
Good Day Bad Day	69
Grandpop Finds a Bunch of Weird Crap Arranged on His Sleeping Platform	51

94	Hopeful Contestants
91	Hostile Sphereoids Sharing a Latte
59	In the Future it Will Be Mandatory to Share Your Cheese with Mutants
70	It Was All Butch Hartigan Could Do to Keep from Strangling Flimsy Jimmy
25	It Was Really Hard to Have Fun When the Kretchmyer Brothers Came to Town
65	Just Before the Gates of Heaven
63	Lakeside Pleasures
24	Late for Mass
14	Levatating an Antipasto
50	Little Freddy's First Glass of Skim Milk
67	Local Genius and His Device
13	Man Forcing a Mutant to Sniff His Shoe
37	Men Detecting a Stench
101	Mildly Disturbing Scenario with Tiny Dancer
78	Miracle Cures Through Essence of Toenail
97	Mr. Peebles And Mr. Van Horst, Attorneys at Law
74	Nancy Liked to Hover over the Dining Table, Silently Breaking Vast Amounts of Wind
76	Nasal Shenanigans
80	Nasty Human Fly
82	Never Put A Rat On A Pedestal
99	Nice Day For A Walk In The Park
32	No Pizza Like A Sanctified Pizza
30	Nude Man With Mysterious Object
58	Out of Control Unicyclist
105	Out of Gas
53	Overworked Urinal on the Run
34	Pennsylvania Douche
29	People Rarely Paid Attention When Pointing George Did His Pointing
39	Professor Arnsworth Supports a Tiny Colleague on His Atrocious Tongue...
31	Professor Hugernot Explains His Predicament Before the Grievance Committee
42	Billie Gets to Meet His Real Father for the First Time
107	Really Weird Birthday Party
103	Revolting Rabbit Family with Axe Murderer
95	Saint Van Dookas Comforts the Egg Man
52	Satisfied Aliens
96	Screwed-Up Lawn Ornaments
77	Self-Proclaimed Gurus Pantomiming the Facts of Life for Filthy William
75	She Didn't Know Who They Were, or What They Wanted, but They Were Always There
66	Sheriff Beasthorn Suspects That Henry's Muffin Was Stolen

Simple Ignorance Stares Down A Complex Enigma	45
Sketchy Individual Pursuing the Sphere of Contentment	83
Strange Little Men from Pluto Forced Michael to Do Unspeakable Things	21
Tail End Of The Meat and Meat Byproducts Parade	15
Taming the Legendary Vershklabiter Beast	85
Teaching Mrs. Mussman to Dance	87
Teaching Willie to Drive	35
The Battle Between Good and Not So Good	38
The Feeding of Dr. Abernathy	27
The First and Last Journey of Truth Seekers Anonymous	104
The Stranger on My Toilet	43
The Wilkerson Brothers Always Had Somethin' Special Goin' On	89
Throwing out a Rat	92
Timmy Finds Two Other Timmys Living in His Sock Drawer	88
Trouble in The Vestibule	9
True Love Knows No Boundaries	81
Twenty Seconds Before the Big Bang	84
Waiting for Traffic	26
Weird Walkin' Stalker Escaping the Law	86
When You've Finally Disappointed Everyone, There's Always the Fetal Position	79
Winged Jackass Tormenting a Simple Polyp	12
Your Guess Is As Good As Mine	23

www.ingramcontent.com/pod-product-compliance
Lightning Source LLC
Chambersburg PA
CBHW081347040426
42450CB00015B/3336